P9-BHX-171

FEDERAL WRITERS' PROJECT

AMERICAN GUIDE SERIES

SAN DIEGO
A CALIFORNIA CITY

AMS PRESS

NEW YORK

AZTEC BY DONAL HORD—SAN DIEGO STATE
CÒLLEGE *(Federal Art Project photograph)*

...D E   S E R I E S

SAN DIEGO
A CALIFORNIA CITY

Prepared by
THE SAN DIEGO
FEDERAL WRITERS' PROJECT
Works Progress Administration
STATE OF CALIFORNIA

641604

Sponsored and Published by
THE SAN DIEGO HISTORICAL SOCIETY

1937

Library of Congress Cataloging in Publication Data

Federal Writers' Project. San Diego, Calif.
  San Diego: a California city.

  At head of half title: Federal Writers' Project.
  Reprint of the 1937 ed., issued in series: American guide
series.
  Bibliography: p.
  1. San Diego, Calif. I. Federal Writers' Project.
II. Title.   III. Series: American guide series.
F869.S22F4 1975   917.94'98   73-3660
ISBN 0-404-57904-3

Reprinted from the edition of 1937, San Diego
First AMS edition published in 1975
Manufactured in the United States of America

AMS PRESS INC.
NEW YORK, N. Y. 10003

Grateful acknowledgment is made by the Federal Writers' Project of San Diego to the many persons who have assisted the project in the preparation of this book. Acknowledgment is made especially to Malcolm Rogers, archeologist of the San Diego Museum; John Davidson, curator of the Junípero Serra Museum; Mrs. Winifred Davidson, local historian; Miss Cornelia Plaister, Librarian, and the staff of the San Diego Public Library; and Louis J. Geddes, photographer and authority on Spanish and Mexican San Diego.

PREFACE

SAN DIEGO: *A California City* is one of the publications written by members of the Federal Writers' Project of the Works Progress Administration. Designed primarily to give useful employment to needy unemployed writers and research workers, this project has utilized their experience and abilities in the preparation for the American people of a portrait of America—its history, folklore, scenery, cultural backgrounds, social and economic trends, and racial factors.

Many books and brochures are being written for the American Guide Series. As they appear in increasing numbers we hope the public will come to appreciate more fully not only the unusual scope of this undertaking, but also the devotion shown by the workers—from the humblest field worker to the most accomplished editor engaged in the final critical revision of the manuscript. The Federal Writers' Project, directed by Henry G. Alsberg, is administered by Ellen S. Woodward, Assistant Administrator.

(Signed) HARRY L. HOPKINS
Administrator.

FOREWORD

San Diego has long been in need of a compact, comprehensive guide book which would not only be of aid to the thousands of annual tourists, but also of interest to residents desirous of knowing the full range of San Diego's colorful history. In the past this need has been satisfied either by voluminous works, far too bulky for handy reference, or by small brochures, tantalizing in their brevity.

It is no easy matter to select well from the thousands of relevant and irrelevant facts which have gone into the making of history here during almost four centuries. That so many have been included, and woven into so compact a form, is this book's chief merit, and will far outweigh, I believe, any individual group interests which might be disturbed by particular omissions. The necessity of presenting a close-knit picture of the total scene has been at all times the compilers' principle, and a perusal of this volume must convince the reader of that constant attention.

San Diego is becoming increasingly aware of its historical heritage —the knowledge that it was the birthplace of California. All historical growths have been strengthened by their traditional backgrounds, and San Diego is more than blessed with its centuries of ever-varying cultural influences. This book is a record of all that, as well as of the city's present development and potentialities as a commercial and industrial center. It is for this reason that the Historical Society has undertaken the sponsorship of SAN DIEGO: *A California City*. It has historical, and, we believe, genuine literary value.

The work of the San Diego Federal Writers' Project must not be judged too lightly because this book can be quickly read. In its final form it is the composite effort of many individuals—a cooperative venture—a social undertaking in the finest sense of the word. More than a year and a half was spent in compiling facts, weighing evidence, writing and rewriting the material. That it shows a unity of purpose and an evenness of writing is a credit to the spirit of the whole Writers' Project whose individual members were able to subordinate personal tastes and interests to the accomplishment of a good job.

LEROY A. WRIGHT, President
San Diego Historical Society.

CONTENTS

PREFACE   *vi*

FOREWORD   *vii*

GENERAL INFORMATION   1

THE CONTEMPORARY SCENE   9

THE CITY BY SECTIONS   12

NATURAL SETTING   17

HISTORICAL   21

   1. The Indians   21

   2. The Spanish   24

   3. The Mexicans   29

   4. The Americans   34

ECONOMIC   45

SOCIAL AND CULTURAL   54

CHRONOLOGY   64

LIST OF TOURS   71

TOURS IN THE CITY   72

TOURS IN ENVIRONS   99

BIBLIOGRAPHY   127

INDEX   131

ILLUSTRATIONS

Cover Design by Mallette Dean, Federal Art Project,
San Francisco

Aztec by Donal Hord   Frontispiece
Silver Strand, Coronado, and San Diego   11
Father Junípero Serra   27
The Lopez House in Old Town   33
Old Town, 1869   35
Horton House   43
Fifth Avenue in the 80's   43
An Early Train   47
Glenn Curtiss and his hydroplane   47
Sweetwater Dam   51
Lindbergh Field   51
Building San Diego by Charles Reiffel   55
Coronado Yacht Harbor   59
Playgrounds of Neighborhood House   59
Grace Lutheran Church   61
Serra Museum   73
Theosophical Society Homestead   81
Old Spanish Lighthouse   81
Lily Pond, Balboa Park   87
Waterfront from the air   91
Civic Center   93
Coastline near La Jolla   97
Coronado from the air   97
San Diego Mission   107
Telescope at Mt. Palomar   111
View of Pine Valley   117

MAPS

In and Out of San Diego   x
Old Town   71
Motor Tours 2 and 5   79
Balboa Park   85
Waterfront   92
San Diego County   Inside Back Cover

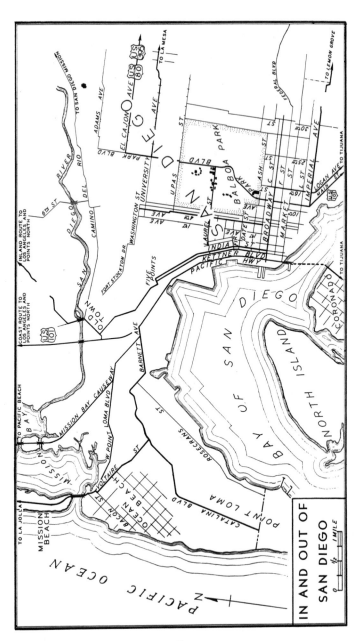

IN AND OUT OF SAN DIEGO

0 ½ 1 MILE

GENERAL INFORMATION

Railroad station: Atchison, Topeka & Santa Fe Ry., Broadway and Kettner Blvd.; downtown ticket offices, Fifth Ave. and B St., four trains daily for Los Angeles and points E., connecting at Los Angeles with the Southern Pacific Lines, for points N.; San Diego and Arizona Eastern Ry. (Southern Pacific Lines), 300 Broadway; one train daily for Calexico, Calif., and Yuma, Ariz., where it connects with trains E.; Union Pacific Ry., ticket office, 345 Plaza.

Airports: Lindbergh Field, Pacific Hwy. and Laurel St., on US 101; United Air Lines and Western Air Express, 5 scheduled flights daily for points N., S., and E.; Airtech Flying Service and Ryan School of Aeronautics, charter and passenger aircraft flights, 2.7 m. from the business district, Third Ave. and Broadway. Streetcar fare, 5c; taxi fare, 1 to 5 passengers, approximately 55c.

Bus lines and stations: Greyhound Lines, 120 W. Broadway, Pacific Greyhound Lines, 28 busses daily, transcontinental service to points N., S., and E.; San Diego Electric Ry., interurban bus service to National City, Chula Vista, Pacific Beach, La Jolla, La Mesa, El Cajon, Spring Valley, and Lemon Grove; National Trailways station, 137 E. Broadway, Santa Fe Trailways and Burlington Trailways, 6 busses daily, through service to out-of-state points N., S., and E.; All American Bus Lines station, 120 W. Broadway, one bus daily to out-of-state points N., S., and E.

Bus terminal for sightseeing trips: U. S. Grant Hotel, between Third and Fourth Aves. on Broadway. Tanner Motor Tours, daily busses to points of interest in city and environs. (See *The City by Sections* and *Tours*.)

Taxis: Several transportation companies provide taxi services. General rates are 20c for the first two-thirds of a mile, 10c for each additional two-thirds of a mile. No additional charge for extra passengers or baggage. Waiting time, $2.50 per hour. Flat rates for rides to suburban towns or places of interest.

Piers: Broadway Pier, foot of Broadway, dock for crafts of U. S. Navy, foreign merchant marine and navies. Pier #1, foot of C St., dock for crafts of U. S. Navy, foreign merchant marine and navies, Hamburg-American (foreign), Johnson Line (intercoastal), Isthmian Line (intercoastal), Luckenbach Line (intercoastal), McCormick Steamship Co. (intercoastal), Nelson Steamship Co. (intercoastal), Quaker Lines (intercoastal), Vancouver & San Diego Navigation Co. (foreign), Williams Steamship Corp. (intercoastal), and Olsen Steamship Co. (coastwise). Ferry slip, foot of Market St., San Diego-Coronado Ferry Co., passenger and automobile transportation to Coronado. (See *Coronado*.)

Star & Crescent Pier, foot of Broadway, tugboat and excursion service.

Sport Fishing Pier, foot of F St., boats for rent.

United Water Taxi pier, 1050 Harbor St., shore boat launch service.

Public buildings: Federal Building, 325 W. F St.; main post office and Federal offices, (new post office, E St., bet. Eighth and Ninth Aves.

open about March 1938) ; public library, 830 E St.; city hall, Fifth Ave. and G St.; county courthouse, 240 W. Broadway; police station, 728 Second Ave.; Motor Vehicle Department, Elks Bldg., Third Ave. and Date St.

Local streetcar and bus service: Urban and interurban streetcar service is provided by the San Diego Electric Ry. Co. The urban area is divided into two zones. The inner zone, S. of Laurel St., and W. of Twenty-fifth Ave., has a 5c fare. A ride through the two zones is 10c. Car tokens are sold on the streetcars, 4 for 30c, each equivalent to a 10c ride. Interurban service and fares are: From Fourth Ave. and Broadway, route L bus, Point Loma, La Playa, three times per hr., 20c one way, 25c round trip; car No. 14-16, twice per hr., Ocean Beach, 20c one way, 25c round trip; Mission Beach, 20c one way, 25c round trip; Pacific Beach, 25c one way, 35c round trip; Bird Rock, 30c one way, 40c round trip; La Jolla, 35c one way, 50c round trip. From Fifth and Broadway, car No. 9, Coronado, 15c one way, 20c round trip, including ferry fare. Weekly passes for streetcar, bus, and ferry use are sold on the streetcars and at the Plaza information booth and the streetcar ticket office, both at Third Ave. and Broadway. Rates for the passes are: San Diego, inner and outer zone, $1.00; first four zones, including Coronado, La Playa, Ocean Beach, Mission Beach, Rose Canyon Road, State College, Seminole and El Cajon Aves., Encanto, and National City, $1.25; first six zones, including Pacific Beach, Bird Rock, La Mesa Heights, and Chula Vista, $1.50; first seven zones, including La Jolla, La Mesa, and the entire system with the exception of El Cajon bus line E. of La Mesa, $1.75.

Law digest: Fish and game laws: Fishing, inland, bay, or ocean, requires a state license; in city reservoirs, an additional daily fee. It is unlawful to fish inland between one hour after sunset and one hour before sunrise. Hunting requires a state license. Information concerning seasons for particular game, fees, and conditions governing hunting is available at the State Fish and Game Commission, R. 201, Broadway Pier.

National Forest Regulations: Maps and special information at U. S. Forest Service, Federal Bldg., F St., bet. Union and State Sts.

1. A campfire permit must be procured before building any fire, including fire in stoves burning wood, kerosene, or gasoline, on national forest land. The nearest forest officer will issue a permit to you without charge.

2. Every camping party in the national forests must be equipped with a shovel and an ax per vehicle or pack train. Shovel, with blade at least 8 in. wide, and an over-all length of 36 in.; ax, not less than 26 in. long over-all, with head weighing 2 pounds or more. Both of these tools to be in serviceable condition. All camping parties will be expected to obtain these tools before entering the national forests.

3. During the fire season smoking is prohibited in the national forests, except in camps, at places of habitation, in special posted areas, and above 7,000-ft. elevation, where smoking is allowed. Smokers must be careful to extinguish their lighted matches, cigars, cigarettes, and pipe heels. Watch for "No Smoking" and "Smoke Here" signs.

4. In periods of high fire hazard, camping and camp or picnic fires may be restricted to posted campgrounds, and part or all of the national

forests may be closed to public use and travel. Watch for "Closed Area" signs.

5. Build small fires. Clear an area down to mineral soil not less than 10 ft. in diameter before starting a fire.

6. Never leave a fire without totally extinguishing it with a plentiful supply of water.

7. Keep your camp clean. Where garbage pits and incinerators are not provided, burn or bury all garbage and refuse.

8. Do not pollute the springs, streams, or lakes by unsanitary acts.

9. Observe the state fish and game laws.

10. Do not mutilate the trees or signs and improvements around camps.

11. Drive carefully on mountain roads.

Wild flower protection: Destructive picking of wild flowers and wild plants within the county is prohibited by a state law and a county ordinance. Scientific bodies gathering for educational purposes may get permits from the County Horticultural Commissioner, County Court House, 240 W. Broadway.

Liquor regulations: No alcoholic beverages are sold between 2 a. m. and 6 a. m. It is unlawful to drive while under the influence of alcohol.

Traffic regulations: The State Vehicle Code is available to the public at the Motor Vehicle Department, 310 Cedar St. Briefly, the speed limits are: 15 m. per hr. when passing school buildings, when the view is obstructed, when traversing intersections or railroad crossings, except upon a through highway or at a traffic controlled intersection; 20 m. per hr. in any business district unless otherwise restricted; 45 m. per hr. under all other conditions. Vehicles must come to a full stop when approaching wholly or partially blind persons carrying a white, or white tipped with red, cane or walking stick, such canes being reserved by law for the blind or partially blind. When driving on roadways which are marked with traffic lanes, a driver should drive as nearly as practicable entirely within a single lane; use the center lane only when preparing to make a left turn or when overtaking and passing another vehicle.

For out-of-state visitors a special traffic slip is used which lists the traffic violations and prescribes as a penalty a visit to three local points of interest, to be selected from the group printed on the slip. When the three have been visited the slip is turned in to the Chamber of Commerce; this constitutes a release.

Parking is permitted on the streets, but restricted in the congested area. There are parking lots throughout the business district that charge by the hour or day.

Accommodations: There are 148 hotels, with 8,740 rooms, chiefly in the downtown area and in Coronado and La Jolla (see *Tours* 5 and 6). Both European and American plan. Minimum rates for one person range from 50c to $10 per day. There are 350 apartment houses, first class, not confined to any particular section of the city. Minimum rents range from $30.00 to $40.00 per month. Forty automobile tourist camps, 10 with trailer facilities, are along the highways at the outer edges of the city. Minimum rates range from $1.00 to $2.50 a day. Restaurants, cafes, and dining rooms offer complete daily menus, with specialties of sea food, Mexican, European, and Chinese dishes. Within a radius of 20 to 70 miles in the San Diego back country are numerous mountain resort areas where tavern and cabin accommodations are available, with rates ranging from reasonable to expensive. The beach resorts are noticeably more expensive during the summer months.

Climate: Rainy season, December-March; dry season, June-September. Average seasonal rainfall for 84 years, 9.74 in.; snow, none; average wind velocity for 63 years, 6.7 m.p.h.; average daily temperature for 61 years, 61.2°; temperature rarely above 90°, rarely below 30°. Usual summer wear clothing is suitable most of the year, though light topcoat should be used in the rainy season and on spring and fall evenings.

Recreation: The following alphabetical list gives the outstanding recreational facilities of the San Diego area.

Aquaplaning: Boards with boats are rented at the boat house, Hotel del Coronado. (See *Tour 5*.)

Archery: An archery club meets every Sunday in Balboa Park, Sixth Ave. and Kalmia St.

Badminton: San Diego Club, 1050 Sixth Ave.; Y. W. C. A., 1012 C st.; Hotel del Coronado, Coronado; State College, 5402 College Ave.; St. Joseph's Roman Catholic Church, Third Ave. and Beech St.

Basketball: Played in season at the Y. M. C. A., Y. W. C. A., Army & Navy Y. M. C. A., San Diego High School, and State College. A municipal league is sponsored by the playground department.

Baseball: Pacific Coast League teams play during season at Lane Field, Broadway and Pacific Hwy. School and amateur semiprofessional teams play at the city playground diamonds. Navy and Service teams play at Navy Field, foot of Fifth Ave.

Boating: Sailboats are for rent at the boathouse, Hotel del Coronado, and at the foot of Santa Clara Court on Mission Bay. Power fishing boats are for rent by the hour, day, or week, with skipper, at the Star & Crescent Pier; at the Municipal Float, foot of Broadway; and at the Sport Fishing Pier, foot of F St.

Boxing: Professional matches each Friday night at the Coliseum Athletic Club, Fifteenth and E Sts. Amateur matches at the San Diego Athletic Club, 1050 Sixth Ave. Service matches at the Naval Training Station and Naval Air Station.

Cricket: Three or four regular games are played annually at Lane Field, Broadway and Pacific Hwy.

Concert halls: Halls available for concerts are Russ Auditorium, San Diego High School; Savoy Theater, 236 C St.; and the Chamber of Commerce Auditorium, 499 W. Broadway.

Croquet: At the Roque Club, Balboa Park, where equipment is furnished.

Discs: A locally developed game closely resembling shuffleboard, played at Shuffleboard Club, Sixth Ave. and Redwood St., Balboa Park.

Excursions on the Bay: Trips daily around San Diego Bay, including visit to North Island. Leave from boat landing, foot of Broadway, and Star & Crescent Pier.

Fishing, deep-sea: (Up-to-date information available at larger sporting goods stores.) Boats leave from foot of Broadway and foot

4

of F St. for barges and boats anchored off the kelp beds near Point Loma and in the vicinity of Coronado Islands, 18 m. out at sea. Private fishing boats may be rented. (Season, May to October.)

Fishing, Mexican waters: (Information as to charter, equipment, license, and conditions is available at Chamber of Commerce, Columbia St. and Broadway.)

Fishing, fresh-water: (Information available at leading sporting goods stores.) Within San Diego County are 10 lakes in which bass, crappie, and occasional trout may be caught during open season, May 1 to October 31. Camping and boating facilities are available at the lakes.

Fishing, surf, bay, and pier: Surf, bay, and pier fishing may be engaged in along the beaches of San Diego County when a state license is obtained.

Football: Southern California Conference games played during the fall at Aztec Bowl, State College; high school games at the City Stadium, Fifteenth St. and Russ Blvd.; and at Hoover High School field, Highland and El Cajon Aves. Service games are played at Lane Field, Broadway and Pacific Hwy., and at Navy Field, foot of Fifth Ave.

Golf: Public or municipal courses are in Balboa Park, 18 holes, near Twenty-seventh and Ash Sts., and Emerald Hills, 18 holes, Broadway Extension. Introduction cards to private golf courses may be obtained at the Chamber of Commerce, Columbia and Broadway. A public pitch and putt course is at Presidio Hills, Old Town. Driving courses are located at Old Town, cor. of Barnett Ave. and Lytton St., and on El Cajon Ave.

Handball: Courts at the San Diego Club, 1050 Sixth Ave.; Y. W. C. A., 1012 C St.; Y. M. C. A., 800 C St.; Army & Navy Y. M. C. A., 500 W. Broadway; and the San Diego Rowing Club, foot of Fifth Ave.

Hiking: At all mountain resorts. Nature walks conducted by the Natural History Museum, Balboa Park, under the guidance of instructors.

Horseback riding: Balboa Park Riding Academy, off Park Blvd., in Balboa Park, level bridle paths along residential district; Mrs. Maupin's Riding Academy, 3800 Twiggs St., Old Town, trails for 50 m. in and about Mission Valley; the Dixie Riding Academy, Sixth Ave. extension, north side of Mission Valley, scenic trails; Cabrillo Riding Academy, Mission Valley at Sixth Ave. extension, trails in Mission Valley and over rolling semiwooded hills; Bar T Ranch, 6104 El Cajon Ave., trails for 50 m. along rolling and flat countryside on outskirts of the city; Joe's Riding Stables, 6202 El Cajon Ave., trails; College Riding Academy, 6244 El Cajon Ave.; Mackey's Riding Club, 2800 Fifty-fourth St., trails through the orange groves; the Coronado Riding Stables, Fifth Ave. and Alameda, Coronado, bridle paths, beach shore riding; Kentucky Riding Academy, Polo Grounds, Coronado, level trails and beach paths; Point Loma Riding Academy, 2074 Catalina Blvd., precipitous bridle paths along Point Loma; La Jolla Riding Academy, La Jolla Shores, constructed bridle paths.

Horse racing: Running events are held at the San Diego County Fair, at Del Mar, in the summer. Racing is available at Agua Caliente, Mexico, 2 m. beyond Tijuana. (See *Tour 6*.) Saddle horse races are run at the Lakeside Rodeo on Labor Day. (*Notable Annual Events*, below.)

5

Horseshoe pitching: Courts in Balboa Park, SE. cor. near Sixth Ave. and Elm St., operated by the Balboa Horseshoe, Chess, and Checker Club. Visitors welcome.

Hunting: Deer, quail, doves, ducks, rabbits, and other small game may be bagged in the San Diego back country. A state license is required. Information is available at leading sporting goods stores.

Lawn bowling: Two lawn bowling greens are located in Balboa Park, Seventh Ave. and Laurel St.

Motoring: Paved and oiled state, national, and county roads lead to points along the seashore and in the mountains and deserts of San Diego and Imperial counties. (See *Tours.*)

Parks: San Diego's system of 24 public parks embraces an area of more than 2,000 acres. (See *The City by Sections: Balboa Park.*)

Roque: Balboa Park, Sixth Ave. and Redwood St.

Rowing: San Diego Rowing Club, foot of Fifth Ave., equipped with all classes of hulls and facilities for mooring of sail and motor boats; Zlac Rowing Club, Ltd. (women), 1111 Pacific Ave., Pacific Beach.

Shuffleboard: Courts in Balboa Park, Sixth Ave. and Redwood St., in connection with the Roque Club, and at Sixth Ave. and Elm St.

Swimming: Ocean and surf swimming along the beaches of San Diego County and Lower California. It is advisable to swim at established centers where life-guards are on duty. Bay swimming is done at Mission Beach, Ocean Beach, and at Tent City, Coronado.

Swimming pools at Y. M. C. A., Eighth Ave. and C St.; Y. W. C. A., Tenth Ave. and C St.; Army & Navy Y. M. C. A., 500 W. Broadway; San Diego Club, Sixth Ave. and A St.; Recreation Area, Balboa Park, at the foot of Texas St.; Mission Beach Bath House, Mission Beach; Ocean Beach Silver Spray Plunge, foot of Narragansett St., Ocean Beach; Coronado Tent City; Del Mar Bath House, Del Mar.

Tennis: Courts maintained by the city are available to residents and visitors at recreation area, Balboa Park, Texas St. (10 courts); La Jolla, Cuvier St. (4 courts, lighted); North Park, Idaho and Lincoln Ave. (2 courts, lighted); Golden Hill, Twenty-sixth St., in Balboa Park (6 courts); Memorial, Twenty-eighth and Logan Ave. (4 courts); and courts at the public schools open to the public after 3 p. m.

Theaters: There are 20 motion-picture houses in San Diego and vicinity, 13 of them being in the main business area. Legitimate stage and musical events are held at the Savoy Theater, 236 C St.

Volley ball: Courts at all municipal playgrounds; also at Y. W. C. A., Tenth Ave. and C St.; Army & Navy Y. M. C. A., 500 W. Broadway; and the San Diego Club, 1050 Sixth Ave.

Wrestling: Professional matches at the Coliseum Athletic Club, Fifteenth and E Sts. Amateur matches are held at the Coliseum once a month, and infrequently at the Naval Training Station.

Yachting: The public yacht landing is at the foot of Ash St. A public boathouse is at Hotel del Coronado. A New Year's racing regatta is held annually the first week in January. (Yacht clubs are listed in the city directory.)

(For other aspects of recreational activity, see *Social and Cultural.*)

Shopping: The business and shopping district of San Diego is bounded on the W. by First Ave.; on the N. by B St.; on the S. by Market St.; and on the E. by Twelfth Ave. It centers around Fifth Ave. and Broadway. Outlying trade areas have developed within the city limits which supply most needs of the nearby residents. Among these districts are Mission Hills, North Park, and East San Diego. Wholesale produce markets are in the district S. of Market St. Retail produce and grocery markets predominate along Twelfth Ave., between Market St. and Broadway. Fish markets are along the waterfront near the foot of Broadway. Mexican stores specializing in native foods are found in the south side of the city, particularly along National Ave. Japanese and Chinese restaurants are in the vicinity of Fifth Ave. and Market St. Curios of Spanish, Mexican, Monterey, and Early California motif are sold throughout the downtown area and at Old Town. Second-hand book shops are on Broadway between Seventh and Eleventh Aves. Tijuana, Mexico,. 16 m. S., is a duty-free port of entry, and merchandise up to $100 in value may be brought across the border free of duty by any U. S. citizen provided it is not for commercial purposes. (See *Tour* 6.)

Street order and numbering: Broadway, running E. and W., is the main thoroughfare. Starting at the bay (W) there are 10 streets, miscellaneously named, followed by a series of numerically named avenues. From A St. (3 blocks N. of Broadway), the streets to the S. are: A, B, C, Broadway, E, F, G, Market St., J, K, L, and Imperial Ave., on the southern water front. North of A St., the streets are named for trees, alphabetically from Ash to Upas. Streets running E. and W. are numbered from First Ave., by 100's, those to the W. of First Ave., running to the bay, those to the E., running to the city limits. Streets running N. and S. start numbering by 100's, at the southern waterfront and continue to Mission Valley on the N. of the city.

Notable annual events: January: New Year's Day Regatta, San Diego Yacht Club; New Year's Day Splash, San Diego Rowing Club.

February: Encinitas National Midwinter Flower Show; Washington's Birthday Regatta, Southwestern Yacht Club; Chinese New Year celebration.

April: Chula Vista Community Flower Show; Mount Helix Easter Sunrise Service; Spring Flower Show, San Diego Floral Society.

May: Felicita Pageant, Escondido; International Salon of Photography; *Cinco de Mayo,* Mexican celebration; Portuguese Festival, Pentecostal Week.

June: Model Yacht Regatta, sponsored by the San Diego *Union;* Junior Olympics, sponsored by the *Evening Tribune.*

July: Coronado Horse Show; Southern California Art Salon; Oceanside Ruff Water swim; Lakeside Rodeo; Annual Tennis Tournament, La Jolla.

August: La Mesa Flower Show; Spreckels Club Golf Tournament, Coronado; Southern California Art Salon, Fine Arts Gallery, Balboa Park; A. A. U. Southern Counties Championship Swimming Meet.

September: Fall Flower Show, San Diego Floral Society; Grape Day, Escondido; Mexican Independence Day (Sept. 16).

October: San Diego County Fair; San Diego County Horse Fair; Navy Day.

November: Armistice Day Annual Football Game; Turkey Day, Ramona.

December: La Jolla Open Golf Tournament, La Jolla Country Club.

Information service: San Diego Chamber of Commerce, Housing Bureau, Apartment and Auto Court Bureau, 499 W. Broadway; Travelers' Aid, Santa Fe Depot, Broadway and Kettner Blvd.; Plaza Information Booth, San Diego Electric Ry., Third Ave. and Broadway; Mr. Foster Travel Service, U. S. Grant Hotel Lobby, Third Ave. and Broadway; Better Business Bureau of San Diego, 402 Southern Title Bldg., 948 Third Ave.; A B C Travel Bureau, 232 E. Broadway; Medical Information Bureau, Medico-Dental Bldg., Third Ave. and A St.; First National Bank Travel Bureau, 1007 Fifth Ave.; and the San Diego Trust and Savings Bank Travel Bureau, Sixth Ave. and Broadway.

THE CONTEMPORARY SCENE

San Diego (0-500 alt., 170,000 pop.) is a loosely knit community of residential districts, business centers, and suburban towns covering 96 square miles of seashore, canyons, and mesas. Climate is its main product; tourists are its principal customers. Its excellent harbor, one of the finest natural harbors on the Pacific coast, has been instrumental in attracting three important contributors to its economic welfare. The fishing industry, operated by the Portuguese and Italians, is the oldest; but in recent years the United States Navy and the aircraft industries have been increasingly active. Tourists visit San Diego the year round, but during the fall and winter months, August through March, is the heaviest traffic. Near the northern boundary of the San Diego metropolitan area is La Jolla, an exclusive residential beach town. Along the seashore are several ocean resorts and amusement centers, focused about Mission Bay. At the northern end of San Diego Bay is Old Town, where California civilization began.

At first glance San Diego's appearance seems to belie the figure of its population. There is little of the hurly-burly, the noise, and the mad scramble of traffic—automobile, streetcar, and pedestrian alike—that characterizes the usual city of this size. There is traffic, and it moves, but it moves unhurriedly. The sidewalks are traversed, but there are seldom great clots of people jamming the street intersections. And probably because of the large proportion of elderly, retired persons, who are not able to elude automobiles as well as they once were, the balance of protection on the city's streets is in the pedestrian's favor. Signs instructing the motorist to stop when pedestrians are in the crosswalk mean what they say. Motorists and streetcar operators alike do not attempt to beat traffic signals. These traffic habits, combined with the unusually short blocks—particularly in the downtown area—all add to the characteristically leisurely atmosphere.

Like almost every city, San Diego has its main downtown artery, and, as in many another city, it is called Broadway. Broadway runs due east and west, and divides the city just as definitely as does Market Street in San Francisco. At its lower end it is a wide calm street, flanked by palms spaced at regular intervals, and from the foot of the street at the bay, looking east, the city appears at its best. The clump of newer office buildings, farther uptown, contrasts sharply with the rest of the area, and presents an impressive skyline. The latest addition to this group of buildings, El Cortez hotel, built on the eminence of an abrupt rise north of Broadway, commands a superb view of the tremendous sweep of bay and the peninsula of Point Loma opposite, and sets the tone of the new and modern city that is the present San Diego. And yet, beginning just a few blocks north, a great mass of green marks the beginning of Balboa Park (1,400 acres), huge and sprawling, much of it as uncultivated as it was on the day the tract was set aside for its present purpose. Around its boundaries the northern half of the city has grown. One of the first exclusive residential districts, Golden Hill, hugs the park's southeastern

9

corner—an area of wide pleasant streets, with many trees and shrubs standing watch in front of the big wooden houses set back in their well-kept lawns. Along the western edge of the park, extending north and south, are many of the new and smart apartment buildings. Northward and eastward from the park the city stretches back, each year spreading farther and farther from the bay.

Immediately south of Broadway is one of the play areas of the Navy enlisted man. Hash houses and honky tonks, drinking parlors with jazz bands and tiny dance floors, trinket shops, shooting galleries, and the ever present pawnshop, combine to make "south of Broadway" a distinct area. But there is considerably more to this section than just these characteristic features of any city's tenderloin district. A little farther south are the remnants of a once good-sized Chinatown—a few forlorn restaurants and a scattering of board shacks. Many of the old original business buildings still stand in all their architectural oddity. Then begins the wholesale and manufacturing section—the warehouses, the gas tanks, the fringe of industrial plants along the southern waterfront. Veering eastward, following the curve of the shoreline, the district widens and becomes residential. In this area are San Diego's Mexican and Negro communities. There is nothing particularly picturesque about this southern end of town—the buildings and the houses are old and in need of repair, there is considerable poverty and very little wealth; if any part of the city could be called slum, this is it.

Since 1900 there has existed a struggle between two elements of the San Diego citizenry. The older group, mainly pioneers and their descendants, have been concerned with keeping San Diego a residential city where tourists might be persuaded to come upon retirement from active business. The newer element, businessmen and industrial leaders, have made every effort to promote San Diego as an industrial center. The effort to keep the town basically a resort area has resulted in a top-heavy economic balance, with too sharp a dividing line between those who are economically secure and the large stratum of working people. San Diego's municipal credit, however, bolstered by the 2-million dollar pay roll of the Navy, has always been above average.

San Diego has gone far since its Mexican village beginnings. It still has that touch of easygoing, *mañana* (Sp., *tomorrow*) spirit typical of Latin-American existence, which makes the city unhurried, conservative, and sure of itself. People dress very much as they please, and, to the visitor from other parts of the country where tradition or climate dictates the mode of daily dress, it may appear that the people are haphazard and tasteless in their choice of attire. But San Diego dresses and lives for comfort. It is rare that some of this spirit does not infect the tourist. Those who come for brief visits are frequently uneasy in the face of such unconventional sartorial philosophy; but the departed tourist remembers San Diego—remembers its climate, its real, comfortable feeling of well-being, and above all its beauty of harbor, hills, ocean front, and back country. And tourists do come back to stay.

10

SILVER STRAND, CORONADO, AND SAN DIEGO
FROM THE AIR *(Official U. S. Navy photograph)*

THE CITY BY SECTIONS

1. DOWNTOWN SAN DIEGO

San Diego's principal business district is concentrated in the area from Twelfth Avenue west to the bay and from A Street south to the bay, with the city spreading fan-wise from this tract. Though an attempt was made in 1850 to found a city on this site, its real development did not begin until 1867, when A. E. Horton purchased a thousand acres and laid out the present street plan. (See *Historical: The Americans.*) At first the center was at Fifth Avenue and Market Street, but following the real estate booms of the 1870's and 1880's, the trend was northward until Broadway has become the main artery.

From all directions traffic converges upon the district, with Broadway carrying the bulk of the streetcar lines. The blocks are short and the streets much narrower than the boulevards of the newer sections. Clustered around the downtown center (1937) of Broadway at Fifth Avenue are the city's imposing group of structures: the newer hotels and office buildings which give San Diego its skyline. But in San Diego the old and new still jostle each other, and particularly in this circumscribed section there is a curious composite of architectural styles. A building of the 1870's stands beside a building with the most ultra-modern of fronts; across the street is a three- or four-storied structure of the 1890's, flaunting a belaced shirt front. South of Broadway, especially in the area of Fifth Avenue and Market Street, many buildings of the 1870's are still in use. Between Market and Broadway are pretentious gingerbread ornamented "skyscrapers" of the 1890's, highly praised in their time for beauty and modernity. Two types predominate along Broadway, the hotel and office building style of the 1910's, and the larger Renaissance type building so popular in the boom days of the 1920's. But newer buildings are gradually appearing: the new Civic Center building lies on the bay edge north of the business area and a new post office of splendid architectural design is nearing completion.

The main streetcar terminal is on lower Broadway, at the Union depot, which also handles the traffic of both railroad systems. Broadway is much wider between the waterfront and Third Avenue than in the remaining downtown area. Horton Plaza, between Third and Fourth Avenues, is a lounging place for the elderly retired and the shopper. At Fifth Avenue is the core of a busy retail district, and a majority of the banks, theaters, and larger hotels are located within the radius of a few blocks. North of Broadway flanking the business houses are numerous residences, the vintage of 1890 predominating. South of Broadway, on Twelfth Avenue, is the principal retail produce market district, flanked by a nondescript residential area. South on Third, Fourth, and Fifth Avenues are cheap eating places, pawnshops, third-run movie houses, and the type of small hotel which offers clean beds from 25 cents up. Around Fourth Avenue and Island Street is the small remnant of San Diego's once large Chinatown, and between it and the bay are large warehouses and industrial plants. To the west and south of this area are the wharves and docks of the waterfront.

2. BALBOA PARK

In an area of mesas and deep canyons, bounded by Date Street and Russ Boulevard on the south, Sixth Avenue on the west, Upas Street on the north, and Twenty-eighth Street on the east, is the 1,400-acre tract of Balboa Park. Since 1915 it has been San Diego's most important cultural and recreational center. Park Boulevard (12th Avenue) running north and south, divides the park into two distinct areas. The western side, of approximately 600 acres, is highly cultivated and contains the greatest number of points of interest. Recreational clubs border the southern and western edges, while the central portion has the museums, art galleries, and exhibition buildings of two world expositions. The lesser developed eastern section of the park contains the municipal swimming pool and tennis courts, the municipal golf course, the naval hospital, the city stadium, and the San Diego High School. Great stretches of barren canyon walls, with green and purple sweeps of chaparral, make up most of this area, indicative of the original appearance of this whole region.

On Sundays, city-tired people wander along the winding pathways and roads and gather at the outdoor organ to hear the featured concert. Floral gardens and landscapings, both simple and intricate, add variety to the ever-changing terrain. The collections in the museums and galleries appeal to visitors, who take an interest in the well-arranged displays, aside from their scientific value.

Though the park was set aside as early as 1868, it was not until about 1892 that extensive plans for development were undertaken. In that year a plan for annual tree planting was evolved, and in 1902 more than $10,000 was collected from public and private sources for grading and planting the southwestern corner. Roads, walks, drives, and general cultivation areas were planned, and Golden Gate Park in San Francisco donated many specimens of plants, to which friends in Australia added specimens of eucalyptus, acacia, araucaria, and other subtropical plants. Since the exposition of 1935-36 the park has been in the best condition of its history.

3. MIDDLETOWN

Between downtown San Diego and Old Town, lying to the west of Balboa Park, is a long, narrow strip of low hills and tidal flats which retains the pioneer name of Middletown. In the 1850's, when the first attempt was made to found a city on the present downtown site, a group of Old Town citizens purchased this strip and set up a rival subdivision. Not until Horton's venture, however, did the area attract visitors; but as it lay along the main thoroughfare between the old and the new town, it became a convenient suburban residential district. Wealthy families built homes on the hillsides overlooking the bay. As the new town grew, and the harbor became commercially useful, these families moved farther back into Mission Hills, and along the western edge of Balboa Park. At present the Middletown area is given over to rooming and boarding houses. The main business center is known as Five Points. To the south, near the fish canneries, are the homes of Italian fishermen; and to the north are the residences of many of the employees of the aircraft works, which are on the waterfront. (See *Tour* 4.)

13

4. OLD TOWN

Like a sleepy, dilapidated ghost town forgotten in the swirl of modern industrialism, Old Town lies northwest of Middletown, radiating in its own quiet, nostalgic way a dignity and repose reminiscent of the old Spanish and Mexican regimes. It is only a skeleton of its former self. Many of the comfortable, rambling adobe houses of the early nineteenth century, scenes of gay fiestas, have long since crumbled into the clay from which they were made. The exceptions are few, a small number that the modern age has belatedly rescued from destruction. Occasionally adobe mounds mark the sites of once pretentious homes; but the majority have been cut into lots and covered with small residences and sprawling, ugly auto courts.

Standing in the old plaza, one finds it difficult to picture the town's appearance before progress moved the business interests south. Trees and greenery have taken away the dry, sun-parched appearance of the plaza. The few existing adobe houses have been altered, and frequently not too respectfully. On the outskirts of the town are several fine adobes, which, if not restored within a few years, will become only memories. The inroads of commercialism have proved a serious danger to the many sites which are still privately owned. The past few years have shown an awakened interest in San Diego's past, and already a few of the relics are being saved for future generations; but there is much left to do. (See *Tour 1.*)

5. POINT LOMA

Point Loma, a peninsula 7 miles long, encloses San Diego Bay on the west, and its cliffs, 400 feet high, rising from narrow, sandy beaches, form a natural windbreak which gives the harbor protection from storms at all times. Except for the residential district at the northern end, the several little centers along the shore line, and the Theosophical Homestead on the ridge, the peninsula remains in its wild state. The cliffs are chaparral covered, and deep ravines are eroded into the eastern and western sides. The tip of the point is a United States military reservation, in which is located Fort Rosecrans. At Point Loma post office, formerly known as Roseville, and at the modern subdivision known as La Playa, is the Portuguese colony. (See *Social and Cultural.*)

Point Loma is one of California's historic sites. Here Cabrillo first set foot on California soil; here Vizcaíno held religious services; here the Americans settled and carried on their hide, tallow, and whale-oil industry; and it was here that the American flag was first flown, though unofficially, and many years before the conquest. (See *Historical: The Americans* and *Tour 2.*)

6. MISSION HILLS

On the hills above Old Town, commanding a view of the ocean, the bay, and Mission Valley, is the exclusive and modern residential district of Mission Hills. Thirty years ago this area was given over to small grain farms and olive orchards. Because of the topography of the area, with the prevalence of short canyons and promontory sites, the developers were forced to lay out circular and winding streets. From 1910 to 1925

14

Mission Hills developed most rapidly. Landscaping of exceptional character was planned and executed by Miss Kate Sessions, to whom also is due much of the beauty of Balboa Park. No definite architectural style prevails in this district, though the earlier residences followed what is generally called the California style. Those built during the past decade are distinctly of the modernistic and Monterey styles. Washington Street is the main thoroughfare of Mission Hills, connecting this rather isolated area with downtown San Diego and offering a short cut to the beach towns from East San Diego. A recent traffic survey reveals that Washington Street is one of the busiest in the city.

7. NORTH PARK

Between Mission Hills and East San Diego, in an area surrounding the junction of Thirtieth Street and University Avenue, is a homogeneous unit of San Diego known as North Park, with an estimated population of about thirty thousand. Here, since 1900, a business and residential center has developed which now has two banks, seven churches, several large stores and many small ones, two theaters, and hundreds of homes. Though there has been a tendency to include North Park with East San Diego as a city division, the local business men have steadily refused to let North Park's individuality be sacrificed. Each year they sponsor a celebration which reasserts their right to be considered a distinct city area.

8. EAST SAN DIEGO

Between North Park and Fifty-eighth Street is East San Diego, which was a municipality of the sixth class until 1923, when it voted to be annexed to San Diego. Had the great real estate boom of the 1880's been successful (see *Historical: The Americans*), East San Diego would have been a thriving city in its own right. Promoters swarmed over the brush-covered hills and mesas, grading streets 100 feet wide, laying out parks and home sites, and even planning for a railroad line. The collapse of the boom in 1888 ended this dream of metropolitan splendor. Not until 1901 was another attempt made to develop the area. Reestablished in that year by the City Heights Land and Water Company, East San Diego grew slowly until 1910-11, when a small boom brought investors and home builders. Two successive booms, one in 1915 and another in 1920, brought thousands of residents. At present, with an estimated population of thirty-five thousand, it is a region of comfortable, medium-priced homes. A strong community spirit is manifested by the business men and residents.

Joining East San Diego on the north and extending to bluffs overlooking Mission Valley are the exclusive residential districts of Talmadge Park and Kensington Park. Northeast, in brushy, rugged hills, just outside the city limits, is a favored area for the construction of luxurious homes.

9. ENCANTO

On ground that was once a part of a Spanish rancho used principally for the grazing of cattle, lies the suburb of Encanto (Sp., *charming*), 6 miles east of downtown San Diego on the extension of Imperial Avenue. The tract was laid out in 1893, and during subsequent promotion periods an attempt was made to attract a motion picture colony to this vicinity, in anticipation of which the subdivisions of West Hollywood and Hollydale were platted. This venture soon collapsed. The present population is a little more than one thousand, and the business section consists of a few stores scattered along Imperial Avenue. The surrounding hills are divided into home sites with many gardens, small orchards, and poultry ranches. A distinctive feature of Encanto is the commercial cactus gardens.

10. LOGAN HEIGHTS

Between Encanto and the Golden Hill area is Logan Heights. The subdividers planned the arterial streets to run in a northwesterly to southeasterly direction so that the sun might shine into every room of every house at some hour of the day; but the plan was not followed during later years, and as a result the district is a maze of cross section streets with numerous triangular lots throughout the area. In the 1890's Logan Heights was one of the choice residential districts. Many men and women prominent in present-day (1937) social and civic life were born, reared, and educated in this neighborhood. As San Diego grew, industrial plants located along the bay front, and even moved into the residential sections. As the district was not restricted, many racial minority groups moved in, particularly the Mexicans and the Negroes. The Mexican colony lies between Sixteenth and Twenty-fifth Streets, along Logan and National Avenues. The most important center of Mexican activity is the Neighborhood House, a community social hall, similar to Hull House, in Chicago. The Negro population has two large areas, one centering on Thirtieth Street between Imperial and National Avenues, the other extending from Sixteenth to Twenty-fifth Streets, between Imperial Avenue and the bay. (See *Social and Cultural.*)

11. GOLDEN HILL

Between Market Street and Balboa Park and Sixteenth and Twenty-eighth Streets is the Golden Hill residential district, which for a quarter of a century was the most aristocratic and highly improved area of San Diego. Its attractive features were its closeness to town and the unexcelled view of the bay to be had from the heights. After 1915, when more distant areas became accessible by means of automobile, this section declined somewhat. The original promoters had several novel restrictions for the subdivision. All houses were on large lots and were built 40 feet from the street, so that all might have an unobstructed view. The sale of intoxicating liquors was prohibited, and no barns were allowed. To compensate for this latter restriction, the promoters, to quote a circular of the period, promised "The company will build at a convenient distance, a two-story, fireproof barn, large enough for the accommodation of all. This building will be constructed with due regard to ventilation and all other means necessary to make it a veritable Horse Palace."

NATURAL SETTING

San Diego, the southwesternmost city of importance in the United States, and the first United States port of call north of the Panama Canal, covers an area of about one hundred square miles facing a landlocked natural harbor. The western side of the harbor is protected by Point Loma, a high promontory about 7 miles in length which breaks the ocean winds; and completing the enclosure of the bay, the Silver Strand, a narrow sandspit, extends southeast and south for 10 miles from North Island to its juncture with the mainland. The entrance to the harbor is a narrow channel between North Island and Point Loma. North of Point Loma, along the coast line, is Mission Bay, separated from the Pacific Ocean by a sand bar, Medanos Point; north of the point is a promontory of high sea cliffs on which La Jolla is built.

In the fairly recent past, Point Loma, North Island, and Coronado were actually islands. Sedimentary deposits of the San Diego River, combined with the action of tidal and ocean currents, joined Point Loma with the mainland and threw up a sandy strand between North Island and the southern mainland. The San Diego River flowed alternately into San Diego Bay and Mission Bay until 1853, when a government dike was built across the river flats from the foot of Mission Hills to the edge of Point Loma, which turned the river into Mission Bay, thus preventing river silt from filling the harbor. In the 1860's this dike washed out, but it was rebuilt in the late 1870's. Between Point Loma and the Mexican boundary line the land is principally lowlands and tidal marshlands.

Downtown San Diego is built along the northeastern slopes of the harbor shore, and the elevation gradually increases, climbing into the mesas to the north, northeast, and east. Upon the mesas are various residential and community centers and Balboa Park. To the north the mesas end at Mission Valley, where there is an abrupt drop of from 200 to 400 feet. The elevation of the city varies from a few feet above sea level at the Old Town flats to 822 feet in the La Jolla area.

About 11 miles inland is a sudden change from the mesa lands to a rough, rugged mountain terrain. Lying between the coastal plain and the mountains is El Cajon Valley (350-500 alt.), a boxlike basin, the only large valley in the immediate environs of San Diego. Augmented by numerous stream channels draining the mesa lands, the San Diego, Sweetwater, Tijuana and Otay Rivers are the principal streams of the San Diego area. Like most rivers in southern California, they are usually dry during most of the year, but in the rainy season they frequently increase to flood proportions.

A wide variety of soils exists in the region, predominantly sandy loams, differing widely in texture. In color they range from brown to black, the commonest type in the vicinity of the city being the reddish brown soil generally known as adobe clay. Agriculture in this area is limited by the water supply and its distribution. The availability of irrigation water, obtained from a network of storage reservoirs or pumped

17

from underground sources, plus the nature of the frost areas, more often determines the crops grown than does the character of the soil. Approximately 20 percent of the land in the vicinity of the city is under cultivation.

The mesa lands, upon which the greater part of the city is built, are composed of a marine-terrace deposit, filled with rounded cobblestones. Six to ten inches below the surface is a tenacious clay layer, not easily penetrated by water or by roots. Because of this structure the natural vegetation of the coastal-plain region is greasewood, chamiso, and other low-growing brush, rarely exceeding 6 feet in height. Because of its equable climate and the artificial water supply which allows irrigation, the bay region is able to support large groves of citrus fruits and avocados, and truck garden crops.

The climate is essentially mild, and the prevailing winds from the Pacific rarely exceed a velocity of 5 miles an hour. The atmosphere is clean, sharply purified by the ocean, and free of dust. Official records, kept since July 1, 1849, show that the average mean temperature of San Diego is 61°. Temperature exceeding 90° averages less than 1 hour a year in the city. An absolute minimum of 25° occurred at 7 a. m. on January 7, 1913, breaking a cold record of 24 years. An extreme high of 110° was reached on September 17, 1913. Along the coast, day and night temperatures vary as little as 13°, though somewhat greater variations occur inland. The average annual rainfall at San Diego is 9.74 inches, increasing in the back country approximately 6 inches for every 1,000 feet of elevation. Official photographic records reveal that on the average less than 9 days out of the year are without sunshine. Most of these occur in the summer months, when a high fog hangs over the region, protecting it from the heat.

Along the coast line the annual average humidity is 75 percent, atmospheric moisture increasing during the night. Thunderstorms and hail are rare phenomena, and snowfall has never been officially recorded in the city, though the mountain areas of the back country are sometimes covered in the winter. (See *Tour* 8.)

Despite the sparse native vegetation, San Diego's streets are lined with thousands of decorative shade trees. Palms and eucalyptuses are most common, each of which is seen in many varieties. Even such tropical plants as bananas are grown here, though the climate is not sufficiently hot and moist to produce fruit of a high quality. Bright yellow-flowered acacias, scarlet and pink hibiscus, lacy-leafed pepper trees with clusters of red berries, brighten the private gardens and the streets at all seasons of the year. In Balboa Park more than 600 acres have been converted into a botanical wonderland (see *Tour* 3). In the back country, over the foothills, and in the hundreds of small canyons which surround the city grow a profusion of wild flowers and plants, mainly cacti and succulents; though blue lupine, wild mustard, monkey-flower, yellow mariposa, wild morning-glory, and Spanish bayonet are commonly seen. Native to the bay region is the Torrey pine, which grows on a plateau between La Jolla and Del Mar.

Many kinds of birds, both land and water, are native to the San Diego Bay region. Some of the species are also found in other parts of the United States, but frequently the local variety differs in plumage, diet, and habits. In the city the most common varieties include the blackbird, the finch, the hummingbird, the jay, the lark, and the California mockingbird. In the farming areas of the vicinity, ravens, crows, sparrows, and hawks are commonest. Because of the miles of shore line and harbor frontage and the prevalence of marshy tidelands, water birds are numerous and varied.

Not many animals roam the nearby foothills today, but occasionally a coyote, an opossum, a bobcat, or a raccoon may be seen prowling around the outskirts of the populated areas. There are frogs, toads, lizards, and turtles in the harbor region, and on rare occasions snakes are found, mainly of the nonpoisonous varieties, though rattlesnakes are common in the back country.

Twenty or more varieties of salt-water fish are caught offshore for commercial and sport purposes, the commonest being the yellowtail, the tuna, and the barracuda. Sport fishing boats are numerous, and the summer fishing season attracts thousands of sportsmen to the bay region. An interesting phenomenon of early summer occurs when a small fish, the grunnion, resembling a sardine or small smelt, spawns on the sands during full moon. The San Diego beaches are colorful areas during grunnion hunts. Bonfires are built and torches used, which reflect from the small silver fish and make them more easily seen. The use of nets. or other devices is prohibited by law and the usual method is to wade into the shallow water and scoop them by hand onto the beach.

To the east of the city stretches the San Diego County back country. It is a mountainous, semiarid region, approximately 70 by 80 miles square. Within its confines are five distinct geographical regions: coastal, mountain, plateau, desert, and valley. Rising gradually from sea level, the land reaches altitudes of 6,000 feet in the eastern portions of the county, and on the Imperial Valley side drops abruptly to the desert basin below sea level. The mountains are a continuation of the Peninsular Range, the principal mountain chain of Baja (Lower) California, Mexico. The tillable land, mainly a series of terraces, or plateaus, has been estimated by the Government to be more than 500,000 acres.

Fossil sea shells found on the summits of hills and mountains support the theory of geologists that at one time the entire area was a shallow sea. Gradual recession of the beach line occurred, and at a later period the whole region was lifted by volcanic action. It is possible that the Colorado River once flowed across the county and emptied into the Pacific Ocean, near the site of San Diego. The Poway Mesa, south of Escondido, is thought to represent the head of the delta of that prehistoric river.

Few vertebrate fossils have been found in the county, and those few are of a relatively late geologic period. They include remains of a mastodon, a prehistoric horse, a camel, a whale, and an auk of the Pliocene period. The majority of fossils are invertebrate, of marine origin. Ammonites measuring 16 inches in diameter, of the Cretaceous period, have been found on Point Loma. They have been estimated by paleontologists to be from one to 250 million years old. Petrified wood has been found in various places along the coastal plain, and in the mountains overlooking Imperial Valley are deposits of petrified wood and extensive deposits of coral.

San Diego County is reputed to have a greater variety of mineral wealth than any other political division of its size in the United States. More than one hundred minerals have been found, principally precious and semiprecious stones. During the 1870's gold was the most important item in San Diego's mining, but in recent years the production has been slight. In turn, the interest has been concentrated mainly on molybdenum, lithia, graphite, arsenic, feldspar, and the precious and semiprecious gems. Topaz in amber, white, and blue, is produced in abundance, placing the county first in the world in its production. The largest deepblue topaz in the world was discovered here. Another gem, kunzite, has been found in great quantities. Approximately 40 tons of tourmaline have been removed from the Mesa Grande ledge, in the northern section of the county. It has been estimated that since 1901 gems worth more than one and one-half million dollars have been extracted from the county mines.

The San Diego mountains are well wooded and support a great variety of trees and plants. In the Cleveland National Forest (see *Tour* 8), which spreads over almost the entire mountainous section of the county, are forests of pine, spruce, fir, cedar, oak, and elm. On the strip of desert in the eastern portion of the county (see *Tour* 8A), grow many flowers and plants peculiar to the American desert. The typical landscape of the county is the rolling, chaparral-covered hillsides, dusty and dun-colored in the hot summer months, but greener and semiverdant in the winter and spring.

HISTORICAL

1. THE INDIANS

"They are very intelligent Indians, noisy, bold, great traders, covetous, and thievish." With this general summary, Father Palou introduced the San Diego Indians to the Spanish world in his *Historical Memoirs of New California*, written shortly after the first expedition had established a garrison and mission at San Diego in 1769. "All the men are naked and most of them painted," he continues, "but the women are modestly covered in front with woven fibers and behind with skins of animals. They all go armed with their bows and quivers of arrows."

The San Diego area was inhabited by Indians of two different linguistic families. Through the southern part of the county were the South Dieguéños, the North Dieguéños, and the Kamia, all members of the Yuman family. Across the northern part were several divisions of the Shoshonean nation, related to the great Uto-Aztecan linguistic stock, which extended from Montana and Utah down into the Aztec territory around Mexico City. The padres were little concerned with the ethnological affinities of their prospective converts, and usually they named the Indian tribes for the mission in whose territory they were located. Thus, of the Shoshonean nation, two of the tribes are known as the Luiseños (Sp., *of Mission San Luis Rey*), and the Juaneños (Sp., *of Mission San Juan Capistrano*); though in the case of the Cahuillas (Sp., from Ind. *Kawia*, tribal name), and the Cupeños (Sp., *those of the village of Kupa*), the tribal names were used.

The Indian of this region was inclined to be stockily built, with very dark brown skin, a flat nose, and a broad face. Father Font, in his Diary of the year 1776, spoke of the natives found at San Diego as being of the Quemaya (*Kamia*) tribe, and noted, he added, "as being in body vile, ugly, dirty, careless, smutty and flat-faced." Though the majority of existing original reports on the local Indian are derogatory, Father Crespi noted that they were proficient in the mechanical arts and learned Spanish readily. In general he thought them very clever and businesslike. Their businesslike characteristics did not impress Father Font so favorably; he remarked that they were "so ill-mannered that to secure some fish the missionaries have to pay them with beads, or corn . . ." The popular present-day conception of the Indians as shiftless and indolent does not bear up under the opinions of the missionaries and soldiers. Indeed, the local tribes appeared to be particularly belligerent in the face of conquest. Governor Pedro Fages, in a letter of 1787, reported that "this tribe, which among those discovered is the most numerous, is also the most restless . . . and hostile toward us, absolutely opposed to all rational subjection, and full of the spirit of independence." It might be well to remember in passing that on the eastern coast of this continent during these same years the Colonists were fighting for independence, but with more success. Fages adds that "it must not be overlooked that a considerable armed force must needs be at hand in sufficient numbers to repress their natural and crusty pride."

21

The Indians lived in *rancherias* (Sp., *villages*), which were collections of crude huts made of branches and tule grass covered with earth. In the vicinity of San Diego Bay, Father Palou noticed twenty such villages. A distinctive feature of Indian villages throughout southern California was the presence of *temescals* (Ind., *sweat houses*), large huts, almost airtight, in which the Indian men assembled to benefit from therapeutic sweatings, and which it appears they also used for general clubhouses and gathering places.

Clothing, as Palou noted, was scanty. In cold weather garments and caps were made from rabbit fur, and those fortunate enough to be good hunters had deerskin and sea otter furs. Moccasins were worn only while traveling over rough country. Through the greater part of the year, because of the mild climate, little or no clothing was worn; but the lack of covering was compensated by a liberal use of paint and head ornamentation. Personal adornment was most characteristic of the male. Body paint and headdresses of beads and feathers were the most prevalent forms of decoration, though tattooing was practiced by both sexes. In general the male appeared to have a monopoly on cosmetics and beautification.

From the mounds of refuse and debris found near Indian campsites, archeologists have been able to rescue fragments of clamshells, fishbones, arrowheads, and broken pottery, from which it has been possible to reconstruct the living conditions and culture of the Indians. In addition to this source of information, tribal and social facts are derived from the early accounts left by padres and explorers. The Indian has been classified, after consideration of the facts, as having been little advanced beyond a stone age level. Metals were unkown in this region; tools were made of stone, shell, wood, and bone. Among the Yuman tribes pottery was known, but many San Diego County Indians had not learned this craft, according to Malcolm Rogers, archeologist of the San Diego Museum. When the missionaries arrived, the Juaneño tribes, for example, were still using primitive soapstone and sandstone utensils. The bow and arrow was used extensively, supplemented in times of fighting by slings, clubs, spears, and even convenient cobblestones. Along the coast, where fish was an important source of food, the Indians built rafts of logs tied with tule and ventured far from shore.

The California Indians were not squeamish about food. Although vegetable products formed the basis of the year round diet, this was frequently supplemented with small game, such as rabbits, and crows; also to this list must be added mice, snakes, frogs, coyotes, and grasshoppers. It was a matter of great rejoicing when an occasional dead whale drifted ashore. Whole villages congregated at the spot, ate their fill, leaving little but the bones, and then smeared themselves from head to foot with the rancid blubber. The padres have left indelible accounts of the stench that emanated from their charges after such feasts. In the main, however, acorns, wild vegetables, seeds, small game, and shellfish constituted the average diet. Acorns, which were highly prized because they could be stored, were ground into flour and cooked. A great number of the tribal wars were fought over possession of rich acorn groves. In the desert regions where acorns did not grow, the staple food was mesquite beans, the seed of the mesquite bush. Cooking was usually done in a very primitive manner. A hole was scooped in the earth and a layer of stones placed in the bottom. On top of this a fire was built and continued until the stones were heated through. After raking the coals aside, food was placed on the hot surface and the whole covered with earth, making an ideal fireless cooker. Grasshoppers were usually driven into huge pits, over which a fire would be built until they were roasted. Though the Indians were omnivorous by nature, a few foods were taboo, particularly bear, squirrel, mud hen, and wild pigeons and doves.

Tribal organization was almost nonexistent among the San Diego Indians. Order and supervision were a problem of the individual family. Most crimes went unpunished, though tribal action was occasionally exerted in cases of murder. Perhaps the most important and widespread social activity was dancing. Among ceremonial dances were the adolescence rituals for boys and girls, the former including a fire dance. Dances for the seasons were common, and purely ceremonial dances, such as burial rite and eagle killing dances, were found in all tribes. But over and above these traditional and ritualistic dances, the natives indulged in "cool weather" dances, which gave pleasure while affording comfort.

Religiously, the San Diego Indians were extremely difficult to understand. Their legends and beliefs did not follow logical sequence, at least any form of logic comprehensible to the modern mind, but instead seemed to strive definitely toward a pattern of incoherence. Creation myths vary greatly in detail. Animals played a large part in their stories, the bear and the eagle being especially venerated. The bear's skin was supposed to have magical properties. Among the legends an outstanding characteristic is the personification of inanimate objects. A legend of the Indians of the Cuyamaca region explains why three peaks are clustered together, while a fourth stands farther to the south. After a terrific battle between the four, Pine Tree Mountain (Corte Madera) moved to its present location. About one hundred years before the white invasion, a new culture emanating from the north spread among these people. Its beliefs centered about the being of a powerful god called Chinigchinich. This new influence modified the basic beliefs and ritualisms of the indigenous tribes, and, had it not been for the arrival of the Spaniards, the new religion might have become entirely at home in its new environment.

Medicine and religion were almost identical, as among other American Indian tribes. Medicine men attempted to cure sickness by sucking blood from the diseased tissue, by blowing "tobacco" smoke upon the part, or by squirting water or saliva over the patient. The most valuable part of the treatment was probably the rubbing and kneading of the body. They specialized, much as the modern medical profession does, though more variety was displayed, as exemplified by such abilities as rain making, curing rattlesnake bites, and the valuable art of turning oneself into a bear to destroy enemies.

This, then, was the field into which Spain sent soldiers and missionaries, to hold against foreign invasion and to convert to Christianity.

Had the native population been better organized the conquest would have added another bloody chronicle to history; yet, notwithstanding the relatively large number of Indians in the territory (four thousand being the estimated population of the San Diego area), the task of subjugation was accomplished with few disruptions. "In the beginning, the Indians of this port showed themselves very haughty and arrogant," wrote Father Palou; but later in the account he added that "by degrees they came to join the mission."

2. THE SPANISH

When Juan Rodríguez Cabrillo, a Portuguese navigator in the service of Spain, set sail from Natividad, Mexico, in June 1542, he but continued the program of exploration which Hernán Cortés had begun in the 1530's. Cortés had actually touched on the southern tip of Lower California, near the site of La Paz, but adverse conditions forced him to abandon his plans for further voyaging. In 1540 he returned to Spain, where he passed the remainder of his life, and the responsibility of continuing the northwestern explorations devolved upon his successor.

The search for wealth which had motivated so many of the New World discoveries still dominated Spain's policy at this time. Fifty years of exploration and conquest had not disillusioned her; and even in the 1540's her endeavors were colored with the hope that, at any moment, some intrepid voyager would discover territories of infinite riches, or, best of all, discover the famed mythical Straits of Anián, a sea passage to the north of America which would give direct and quick access to China, Japan, and the fabulously rich East Indies.

Cabrillo, with two small, ill-constructed boats, the *San Salvador* and the *Victoria*, was instructed to go as far north as possible, in the hope that once and for all the fact or the fiction of the Anián Straits might be known. The trip was slow and beset with difficulties, but on September 28, 1542, he reached a fine bay. Rounding the protecting point, he entered the harbor, and, as the diary of the voyage states, named the harbor for San Miguel (Sp., *St. Michael*). The diary adds, "being in this port there passed a very great tempest, but on account of the port's being very good they suffered nothing."

Thus Cabrillo was the first white man to enter the harbor of San Diego. After remaining in the bay for 6 days, the expedition continued northward. In October they landed at the island of San Miguel, where Cabrillo suffered a broken arm, but in spite of the pain he resumed the voyage. Storms were encountered during November, which forced them to turn back, and again they anchored at San Miguel Island. Here Cabrillo died as a result of his injured arm. Ferrelo, the pilot of the expedition, took command and returned northward as Cabrillo had desired. On March 1, 1543, he reached the northern limit of this voyage, somewhere off the coast of present-day Oregon. The ships put back for Natividad, reaching port in April.

In the course of the next 60 years several voyages were made along the coast, notably those of Gali in 1584 and Cermenho in 1594, but there is no record of another visit to San Diego harbor. Francis Drake's discovery of Drake's Bay in 1579 and his claim of this territory for England under the name of New Albion stirred Spain to an awareness of the danger to Mexico should a foreign power secure a foothold in such near territory. Already the freebooting of Drake and Thomas Cavendish, the plundering of the rich Manila galleons, made it desirable that ports be established in California where these ships might touch before making the final stage of their voyage to Mexico. The capture and looting of the galleon *Santa Ana* in 1587 by Cavendish brought matters to a head. The government turned its attention to the problem of finding a port of safety on the northwestern coast. Several false starts were made, but on May 5, 1602, three ships sailed—the *San Diego,* the *Santo Tomás,* and the *Tres Reyes*—under the leadership of a merchant navigator, Sebastián Vizcaíno. From the tip of Lower California, each mile of coast line was mapped and charted, the bays and points given names, and careful observations made.

It was on November 10 that Vizcaíno dropped anchor in the harbor of San Diego, which no one had entered since Cabrillo's expedition. Everyone was charmed with the situation, and after preliminary observations, a camp was established on Point Loma headland. On November 12, the feast day of *San Diego de Alcalá* (Sp., *St. James of Alcala,* St. Didacus of the Roman Catholic Church), patron saint of the flagship, a solemn mass was said, and the bay was named in his honor. For 10 days Vizcaíno's men explored the surrounding area and scraped and overhauled their ships, after which the northward journey was continued. Monterey Bay was entered, and Vizcaíno wrote highly of it; in fact, he decided that in spite of his former belief that the bay of San Diego was the ideal port for the Manila fleet, Monterey was better.

Vizcaíno's voyage was a success so far as the objectives of the trip were concerned. The voyage had been difficult. Men suffered from the severe ocean storms, and, worst of all, from the poor food. Scurvy, so often a companion of the early navigators, plagued the small band. Before they reached the home port, more than 40 had died of the sickness. "The sick were dying of hunger because they could not eat what was on board the ship on account of their sore mouths," Vizcaíno recorded in his diary.

Though the voyage was successful, the knowledge gained from it was never properly utilized. Before Vizcaíno's reports were inspected by the Spanish authorities, a new viceroy arrived in Mexico, whose subsequent actions nullified the benefits derived from Vizcaíno's explorations. Again the will-o'-the-wisp report of fabulous riches, this time of islands between the west coast and Japan, stirred the Spanish officials. It was decided to abandon the proposed settlement at Monterey and to divert the funds into an expedition to find the mysterious islands. Not until 167 years later did white men again enter San Diego harbor.

In the late eighteenth century, Russia began an intensive exploration of the Alaskan country, and Russian hunters and explorers moved slowly but steadily down the western coast. Spain awakened suddenly to the fact that Monterey Bay was in danger of being colonized by a powerful foreign nation. A few missions had been established in Lower California, but this was the extent of the Spanish frontier in the Californias. Luckily for the Mexican government, it had an energetic inspector general in José de Gálvez, who, in 1768, made extensive plans for the immediate colonization and fortification of San Diego and Monterey. From La Paz, Gálvez personally supervised the expeditions which were to go north, three by sea and two by land. The *San Carlos* sailed on January 9, 1769, with 62 members in the crew. On the 15th of February the *San Antonio* sailed. It arrived in the port of San Diego on April 11, but there was no trace of the *San Carlos*. With a crew weakened from scurvy, the *San Antonio* waited for her sister ship until the 29th. On that day the *San Carlos* arrived, hardly able to get into port because of illness in the crew, 24 having already died of scurvy. A third ship, the *San José*, never reached port nor was it heard of again.

Gálvez turned his attention to the land expeditions. Under the command of Captain Rivera y Moncada, a company of about seventy, including Father Crespí, had marched north. They arrived on May 14 and found the disastrous conditions existing on the two ships. Fortunately for the crews, Rivera had brought fresh food with him and more than four hundred domestic animals. The whole company settled down and awaited the arrival of the final party headed by Portolá, governor of the new province. On June 27, Sergeant Ortega pushed ahead of the main body and informed the miserable settlers at San Diego of the nearness of Portolá. Rivera sent an escort of 10 soldiers to meet him, and Portolá hurried into camp, arriving on June 29. The rest of his party, accompanied by Father Junípero Serra, father president of the California missions, arrived before noon on July 1. There was great rejoicing in the camp. Medical supplies had come with the land expeditions, and the presence of their governor and commander in chief, Portolá, heartened everyone. Plans were made to establish a garrison and a mission, and Portolá determined to select a small band and push on to Monterey, the main objective of his trip.

The first years of San Diego's existence as garrison and mission were miserable. Serra built a small hut on July 16, 1769, on the edge of a hill overlooking the river flats at the head of the bay. Here a solemn mass was said, and the first mission of Upper California was established to the glory of God and the conversion of the heathen. It was named Mission San Diego de Alcalá, in honor of the patron saint for whom Vizcaíno had named the district. Earthworks were thrown up around the church area, and after the building of huts for the use of soldiers and for supplies, it became the first presidio of Upper California.

Conversions came slowly for the padres. In 1773 Fathers Crespí and Palou arrived to assist their old friend Serra. By 1774 it was evident that the site selected was unsuited for a mission, both because of the lack of tillable land for planting and because of the nearness of the garrison, which did not set a good example for the converts. The padres moved up Mission Valley about 6 miles, and there in the fall of 1774 ground was broken for a new building.

On the night of November 4, 1775, about four hundred Indians attacked the mission and burned it to the ground. Among the slain was Father Luis Jayme, the first martyr in the California field. Heroic men were these padres, who sacrificed their lives and comfort that Christianity

FATHER JUNIPERO SERRA, WOODBLOCK
BY FRANZ GERITZ

might cover the earth. Jayme, finding that the Indians were destroying the mission, walked out to them, extended his arms, and said, "Love God, my children!" The Indians set upon him with clubs and killed him.

This dreadful set-back did not deter Serra from continuing the work. When he heard of Jayme's martyrdom, he exclaimed, "Thanks be to God! That land is already irrigated; now the conversion of the Diegueños will succeed."

The mission was rebuilt and rededicated in 1777. Vineyards and orchards of olive, date, and pear trees were planted. The herds were set to graze in the fertile pasture lands in the little valleys of the surrounding country, and everything flourished.

Life was slow at San Diego in the succeeding years. Few records have come down, because, the seat of government being at Monterey, San Diego remained only one of the four principal garrisons of the province and the other missions prospered more than San Diego Mission.

The first excitement of any importance to the little village was the arrival of the ship *Discovery*, under the command of the navigator Vancouver, in 1793. Spanish policy prohibited foreign trade with her colonies; but this man came to observe and gather scientific data. His book, published shortly afterwards, described San Diego as a wonderful port, but inadequately protected. He recommended that a fort be placed at the entrance to the harbor, at Point Guijarros (Sp., *cobblestones*). By 1803 this had been done.

The first Yankees to set foot in San Diego were four sailors who had been left in Lower California. They walked to San Diego and arrived in 1798. After being held by the authorities for a while, they were deported to Mexico. The first Yankee ship to enter the port was the *Betsy* on August 25, 1800, and after taking on water and wood it departed, much to the relief of the officials. But in the face of Yankee acquisitiveness this isolation did not last. Reports of the wealth of skins to be had in California had already reached Boston, and during the first half of the nineteenth century the Boston clippers arrived at the California ports in ever increasing numbers.

In 1803 the sailing vessel *Alexander* made an unsuccessful attempt to smuggle five hundred otter skins from the harbor, and later in the year the *Lelia Byrd* had a lively skirmish while trying to smuggle furs. The fight between this ship and Fort Guijarros, in which several shots were exchanged, became the widely talked-of "Battle of San Diego."

In 1813 the Mission San Diego in its new and final form was dedicated. The present restored mission represents that stage of its existence. (See *Tour* 7.) During these years the converts increased in numbers, and about 1818 it was found advisable to establish an *asistencia* (Sp., *chapel*) at Santa Ysabel, 40 miles inland, to take care of the many Indians who could not keep in close contact with the mission.

In 1818 there was a flurry of excitement when it was feared that Hippolyte Bouchard, a pirate flying the outlaw flag of Buenos Aires, would raid San Diego and destroy the garrison. Bouchard had already looted Monterey and had moved on San Juan Capistrano. From San Diego, Santiago Argüello led a party of 30 men to the aid of San Juan, but Bouchard landed, seized some food and wine, and sailed away. He ignored San Diego on his way south, which might indicate that he was aware that the port was too poor to repay an attack.

The garrison was occasionally augmented with fresh soldiers from Lower California, but rarely during the Spanish rule were they paid, though nominally they received a salary. Food and clothing, neither very plentiful, came from the mission supplies. The population of the *presidio* in 1820 was about 450 persons, 175 of whom were members of the military. During this time the community became increasingly lethargic. No one seemed to mind the steady deterioration, though reports were sent to Mexico accompanied by requests for funds for rebuilding and repair. Even the former vigilance in regard to the intruding of foreign craft relaxed; and when the British whaler *Discovery* entered the harbor in 1820 and took soundings there was no objection from the *comandante* (Sp., *commander*).

In Mexico in the second decade of the nineteenth century there were rumblings of rebellion against the Spanish rule; but little San Diego was too far out of the world to be either concerned with or to know much about what was happening. Spain was losing her Mexican colonies, but to San Diego the whole problem was how to get food and clothing and what to do about the dilapidated condition of the garrison buildings. In Mission Valley the padres did their best to make the mission as self-sustaining as possible, for they too had long before that time ceased to expect much aid from the mother country.

3. THE MEXICANS

California from its earliest days until the advent of American rule had of course never been more than an outpost of Spanish civilization. By 1800, Spanish authority had so visibly weakened in her American colonies that during the following two decades her possessions one after another declared themselves independent. Mexico after 1810 was a hotbed of political disturbances, yet few of these revolutionary movements affected the *presidios* and *pueblos* (Sp. *garrisons* and *towns*) of California. For many years the military of the California garrisons had been forced to live on the products of the missions, giving bills of credit against the Spanish crown for the goods received. Though the padres had little hope of being able to redeem these notes, and though they did not relish the task of caring for the white population as well as for the Indians, they were helpless in the face of the armed force which the military commanders could bring to bear against them. It was not an uncommon thing for the commander to march to a mission and take by force the grain his troops needed.

Neglected as they were by the home government, the Californians were compelled to depend upon their own resources. This fostered a feeling of independence which was later to make theirs a troublesome province for the Mexican officials. The successful revolt of the patriot-priest Hidalgo in 1810, which freed Mexico from Spanish rule, and the subsequent crowning of Iturbide as emperor of Mexico in 1821, were already old events when the Californians heard of them. The Californians were puzzled, but swore allegiance to the new government, ex-

29

pecting no worse treatment than the old one had given them.

In April 1822 the Spanish flag was replaced by the new Mexican emblem; and before the year was out California's first gubernatorial election had been held and Luis Argüello elected. After the excitement died down, the people returned to their cattle raising, *fiestas,* and dull *presidio* routine as though nothing had happened. In 1825 José María Echeandía was appointed governor. Because his territory included both Upper and Lower California, he chose San Diego for his capital. Naturally, there was dissatisfaction in Monterey, the actual capital of the province, but Echeandía continued to reside at San Diego, contending that its climate was better for his health. Monterey attempted a revolt, which Echeandía quelled, but the disturbances forced him to pass the greater part of 1829 in the north. His enemies hinted that San Diego's chief attraction for the governor was the gay *señoritas.* But San Diego flourished under his administration, and the port revenues for 1828 were $34,000, the greatest in San Diego's history before American rule, and 6 times that of the port of San Francisco.

Throughout this period cattle raising was the mainstay of California economics. Because the white population was mainly military, and therefore confined to the presidial areas, it was not an easy matter to cultivate intensively the rich outlying lands, but cattle turned to graze in the open valleys and on the hillsides could be looked after by a few *vaqueros* (Sp., *cowboys*). Soon the leading families of the state were cattle barons, owning great tracts of land which were usually granted to them by the government and on which they pastured thousands of head of cattle and horses. The mission system broke down under Mexican rule, for though in theory the mission lands were held in trust by the government for the Indians, in practice they were given away to political adherents, with little observance of the rights of the natives. True, it was stipulated in most of the grants that the new owners should consider the Indians as wards and should not interfere with their territorial usage. As long as the lands were held by Spaniards and Mexicans, the Indians were accepted as part of the responsibilities of the *rancheros* (Sp., *ranchers*), but when the Americans came and bought the *ranchos* (Sp., *ranches*), most of the Indians were driven into the uninviting and almost unproductive areas of the back country.

The cattle production of California became known to shipping interests in the eastern United States, particularly those centered in Boston. The *Sachem,* visiting San Diego in 1822, is generally credited with opening the hide trade, which in the succeeding years made the *rancheros* prosperous and, of course, added greatly to the material wealth of the United States. San Diego became the base of operations for most of the hide-carrying vessels, and hide houses, rude, barnlike structures, were built at La Playa, under the shelter of Point Loma. Here hides were cured and stored until taken to the east coast. Richard Henry Dana, Jr., in *Two Years Before the Mast* describes the time that he passed at San Diego and along the coast in this trade. Though the hide traffic became of great importance, it had not been gained easily. The Spanish policy of keeping all ports closed to commerce with foreign ships was for the most part done away with under Mexican rule, especially because of the opportunity to charge for licenses and to lay import duties, for the California-bound ships brought merchandise that was sold and traded for the hides and tallow. Import duties were high, and the Yankee traders smuggled whenever possible. All ships were required to clear at Monterey, but more often than not the captain of a ship, having paid duty at Monterey, would transfer the cargo from one or more sister ships, and thus trade and sell several shiploads for the price of one license. These ships brought woolen and cotton stuffs, agricultural implements, firearms and powder, hardware and feminine toilet articles. The ships' decks were used for display counters, and the arrival of a merchant ship was hailed as a gala event. The Californians would pour down to the harbor to buy what they needed; and then, as now, it was human nature to look without buying.

Though trade restrictions were few under Mexican rule, the government did not overcome its fear of foreign intervention and conquest. For this reason all foreigners in the country were watched carefully. Many of the traders remained in California, settled down, took out Mexican naturalization papers, became Catholics, and married into Spanish families. But any new adventurer landing on the shores or coming overland was treated as an enemy until his actions should prove him otherwise. The Jedediah Smith party, coming overland in December of 1826, received brusque treatment at first, but after being examined by Governor Echeandía at San Diego they were allowed to obtain supplies and go about their business. In 1827 Duhaut-Cilly, a French sea captain, visited the port and described San Diego as a ruined *presidio,* ill-shapen and ugly, with 30 or 40 mud houses on the river flats. In the following year the Sylvester Pattie party of eight trappers landed in San Diego. Echeandía, according to the account published in after years by Sylvester's son, James Pattie, was cruel and unbending in his suspicion of these Americans. Sylvester died in the presidial jail, and the others were released only after James proved that he had a vaccine to combat a smallpox epidemic that was raging throughout California. Though *Pattie's Narrative,* published in 1831, is the only source for this account and his veracity has been questioned on many points, the whole account well represents the official attitude toward foreigners.

When Manuel Victoria arrived in San Diego in December 1830, Echeandía's governorship ended. Victoria immediately removed the seat of government to Monterey, where he instituted a high-handed policy of dictatorship. With this move he incurred the enmity of the Californians, who considered themselves practically a separate state with constitutional rights. In the fall of 1831, Abel Stearns and José Antonio Carrillo, both of whom had been banished by Victoria, met at San Diego, and together with Juan Bandini and Pío Pico conspired to oust Victoria. This revolt was one of the first of a series of comic-opera wars which were destined to flare up at a minute's notice during the remaining years of Mexican sovereignty. An army of about 20 men marched on the San Diego *presidio* and captured it, imprisoning the commanding officers. After Echeandía had been convinced that he should head the revolt, and all of San Diego had joined in, a manifesto was issued, and the army marched on Los Angeles. Victoria marched south with only 30 men,

31

not knowing the full force of his enemies. On December 6, the rebels met him in Cahuenga Pass (in modern Hollywood), two hundred strong. A verbal battle started, which wound up in a slight skirmish in which two men were killed and Victoria was wounded. Echeandía's force, despite its outnumbering Victoria's almost 7 to 1, fled the field. A few days later the iron-handed but sincere Victoria, after thinking the situation over in the quiet cloisters of San Gabriel Mission, resigned. Echeandía resumed office, and when a legislative body met, Pío Pico was elected governor. Echeandía did not approve of this, and after Los Angeles refused to recognize the new ruler, Pico resigned, having governed only 20 days. Echeandía and Agustín V. Zamorano then ruled jointly until a new governor was appointed by Mexico.

José Figueroa, the new appointee, arrived at Monterey in January 1833. His rule was better than that of the previous governors, but it was unfortunate that he was required to complete the secularization of the missions. By this act thousands of Indians were forced away from the protection of the church, at a time when they were not equipped to compete in the white man's way of living.

In 1834 San Diego was organized as a *pueblo,* and Juan María Osuna became the first *alcalde* (Sp., *mayor*). After 1836 the town's population decreased, and in 1838, not having the requisite number of citizens to constitute a *pueblo,* the council resigned and San Diego for the next 8 years was ruled as a department of Los Angeles. By 1840 the population was scarcely more than one hundred and forty persons, and the *presidio,* which boasted but one soldier the year before, was now a crumbling heap of ruins. Save for an occasional Indian uprising in the back country, the town's lethargic existence was unruffled. It slept quietly beside the bay, hardly aware of the constant political bickerings in the northern part of the state. In 1837 Juan Bandini attempted another revolution, this time against Gov. Juan Bautista Alvarado, but after capturing Los Angeles he hurried home to quell an Indian uprising. The Indians subdued, he assembled his "Army of the Supreme Government," about one hundred men, and marched north. Then followed a typical musical-comedy turn. Mexico, having established a new government, sent a commissioner to the Californias with the laws of 1836 to replace the old constitution of 1824. He stopped at San Diego, where the citizens took the oath of allegiance to the new laws. The commissioner joined the revolutionaries at San Luis Rey and marched with them to Los Angeles. In Los Angeles they held a *fiesta,* and everyone took the oath. In the meantime, Governor Alvarado marched south to meet the insurgents and, being met in Los Angeles by the commissioner, took the oath of allegiance to the new laws. This left the rebels without a revolt, for the old enemy was now on their side. The "supreme army" melted away, and Alvarado returned to his gubernatorial duties. Somehow the southern faction felt that they had been cheated out of a good revolution, but there was nothing that could be done about it.

Declining San Diego had another small glimpse of Mexican grandeur before dropping out of the political picture altogether. Gov. Manuel Micheltorena arrived to take command in California, bringing with him an army of about five hundred convicts. This was Mexico's

THE LOPEZ HOUSE IN OLD TOWN, TYPICAL OF THE
MEXICAN PERIOD *(Geddes photograph)*

way of getting rid of criminals and at the same time of fortifying the
California frontier against a possible revolt. The recent loss of Texas to
the Americans was fresh in Mexico's mind. San Diego, which had hailed
with delight this break in the monotony of its existence, was only too
glad to see the last of Micheltorena's vandals. Alfred Robinson, an early
American settler, who was in port at the time, described the situation.
"Day after day the place resounded with the noise of the trumpet and
the drums; and a level spot, on the river's margin, was the scene of
military maneuvers. At night, the gardens and vineyards were plun-
dered, and the neighboring farms suffered greatly, from the frequency
of the soldiers' visits."

Micheltorena's rule and his army were thoroughly disliked. In
1845 Pío Pico and a force defeated him at Cahuenga Pass, and the governor agreed to leave California and take his army with him. Pico
assumed power and removed the capital to Los Angeles, leaving José
Castro as military commander at Monterey with power to collect customs
receipts. In the midst of this divided condition, Pico foresaw the beginning of the end of Mexican rule. Realizing that California would probably throw off her allegiance to the mother country, he used the last few
months of his power in granting thousands of square miles of California
lands to himself, his friends, and his followers. Many of these grants were
near San Diego, the largest of them, Rancho Santa Margarita, of 133,400
acres, he granted to himself and his brother Andrés. The validity of
these land grants occupied the United States Land Commissioners for
many years.

In 1846 the long-expected uprising of foreigners occurred. The

33

bear Flag Revolt, under John C. Frémont, established an independent republic, in part of the territory at least; and before this could be overthrown, the war between the United States and Mexico broke out. On July 29, 1846, the American sloop of war *Cyane* sailed into San Diego harbor under command of Capt. Samuel F. Dupont with a company of about one hundred and sixty men, including Frémont, Kit Carson, Alexis Godey, and a few Delaware Indian scouts. Many of the leading citizens welcomed them, and amid festivities on their part and uncertainty on the part of the rest of the population, Lieutenant Rowan raised the American flag in the plaza. Thus ended Mexican rule in San Diego, though in actuality the little town remained thoroughly Mexican in appearance and temperament for several decades.

4. THE AMERICANS

Cahuenga Pass, which for years had been the Armageddon for so many California conflicts, saw also the termination of the war between the United States and the Californians. There, on January 13, 1847, Gen. Andrés Pico surrendered to Frémont, bringing an almost bloodless war to a close. Although the war lasted about 6 months, and the skirmishes were mostly hide-and-seek games between the opposing forces, one battle, at least, that of San Pasqual, in December of 1846, was of dramatic import.

After the flag of the United States had been raised in the plaza of Old Town, in July of 1846, Frémont and Stockton waited 10 days before they marched against Los Angeles. The Mexicans proved restless, and because of the smallness of the American garrison left to hold San Diego, they mustered a force and attacked the town. The Americans, together with a few of the Californian families who had favored the American occupation, fled to the whaler *Stonington,* anchored in the bay. Again the Mexican flag flew over the plaza. Captain Merritt, in command of the American force aboard the *Stonington,* decided to retake the town. Fearing that the old cannon of the *presidio* might be used against his men, he dispatched Albert B. Smith, a sailmaker who had lived for some years in San Diego, to spike them. With that accomplished, his force marched on the town, engaged the Mexicans, and drove them out. Smith, under fire, climbed the flagpole to attach the halyards, and then hauled the United States flag into place.

In November, Commodore Stockton returned to San Diego and relieved the city from the Mexican forces which continued to harass the inhabitants. Not to be surprised again, Stockton ordered the fort on the hill strengthened and added a hundred men to the garrison. In the meantime, Los Angeles had been recaptured by the Mexicans, and Stockton prepared to march north again. Before he left San Diego, however, he received a communication from Gen. Stephen Kearny, stating that he was approaching San Diego, guided by Kit Carson, and that he was bringing additional forces to assist in the ·conquest. He had left Fort Leavenworth, Kansas, under orders from President Polk, and his men and horses were exhausted from the long desert crossing. On December 5, a detachment of Stockton's men met Kearny's command near Santa

OLD TOWN, 1869, PHOTOGRAPH BY RUDOLPH
SCHILLER *(Geddes photograph)*

Ysabel. Kearny sent out a scouting party which found the Mexican forces, under command of Gen. Andrés Pico, camped near the Indian village of San Pasqual. In the night Kearny marched against the enemy; and, in spite of the pouring rain, the undernourished men and horses, and the ill-advised tactics of attacking an enemy in strange territory without knowing his size and strength, Kearny decided on a surprise attack and advanced upon the enemy position at dawn, December 6. His advance guard came over a hill and sighted the campfires of the Californians. Without waiting for the rear guard, and with little intelligent planning, the detachment was commanded to charge. The Californians, seeing the smallness of the American force descending upon them, formed in line and met the charging force upon their lances. The slaughter was brief. After 19 Americans were killed and 16 wounded, the unharmed Californians galloped into the hills and surrounded Kearny's whole force.

Kearny attempted to rally his men, sent frantic messages to Stockton for aid, and moved the detachment as near as possible to San Diego. Constantly besieged by the Californians, he was forced at last to make camp and throw up what fortifications were possible under the circumstances. On December 9, a rescue party of 215 men arrived, and Kearny's shattered force was escorted into San Diego, arriving on December 12. The Californians retired to San Gabriel, where they put up a losing battle, on January 8, 1847. Five days later Pico capitulated to Frémont at Cahuenga.

The period immediately following the war was chaotic and unsettled. The new territory, which officially became a part of the United States by the ratification of the Treaty of Guadalupe Hidalgo of February 2, 1848, was filled with warring factions, demoralized Indians, and stragglers from the east who had begun to arrive even before news of the discovery of gold. After the gold strike at Sutter's Mill, eastern newspapers publicized the country so thoroughly that within a year thirty-five thousand persons had become citizens of the state.

Many of the Spanish families of San Diego were delighted at the change in rule. Such prominent citizens as Miguel de Pedrorena and Juan Bandini would have been executed by Mexico as traitors had the war terminated in a victory for the Californians. Bandini had furnished a horse to Frémont when the Americans began their attack on Los Angeles. Bandini's daughters made the first United States flag flown in San Diego from old flannels and muslins. Pedrorena had stolen one of the presidial cannon and buried it in his back yard to keep it out of Mexican hands.

Among the American troops stationed at Old Town were the Mormon Battalion and Stephenson's Regiment, Company I. Seventy-eight members of the Mormon Battalion were stationed at Fort Stockton, and diaries of various members of the detail record their activities during that time. One soldier wrote that he had "whitewashed all San Diego." A son was born to the wife of Capt. Jesse D. Hunter, commander of the Mormons, and was named Diego, in honor of the town. He is reputed to have been the first child born of American parents in San Diego.

In some cases troops were stationed in private homes, as is evidenced by a letter of Juan María Osuna, first Mexican mayor of San Diego, which is now in the files of the Serra Museum. The letter, in poor Spanish, lists the damage done to his house by the soldiers, and is translated as follows:

"List of the damages suffered by my house during the occupation of the town of San Diego, the year 1846, my house having been used as military barracks.

"First: an orchard attached to the house, with the chili and onion garden; a cased water-well, and its superstructure. All of this was destroyed. They filled up the well. All of the wooden fence was split into kindling. The value of all this is one hundred pesos.

"They threw down a section of the wall of the afore-mentioned orchard, to make a fortification: $32. Within the house (there was taken) from the pantry, 225 pounds of salt; 15 strings of chili; 12 (strings) of onions; and two containers of onions. The value of the salt, $18; of the chilis, $11.25; of the onions, $24; and of the two containers, $10; one table, $7; the double doors of the cupboards, which were also converted into kindling, $4; the boards of the closets, $2; the large-sized adobe (bricks) which they destroyed, $3; one dozen spoons, $3; a pitcher, $1; a night-pot, $1; and two jars of lard, $10.

    Feb. 15, 1847.   (signed) *Juan Ma. Osuna.*"

In 1847, the first official census of San Diego County was taken by order of Colonel Stephenson. The white population numbered 248; and there were 483 converted Indians, 1,550 "wild" Indians, 3 negroes, and 3 Sandwich Islanders. In September of 1848, the Stephenson Regiment was mustered out; but detachments of other regiments were stationed at the San Diego Mission until late in the 1860's.

Because Congress was too busy with the slavery issue to pay much attention to the new territory, California was left to shift for itself. Lawlessness abounded, and as Cleland states, in his history of the American period, "There was Civil Law, Pike County Code, New York Code, Common Law, Maritime Law, Law of the Plains, Military Law, and Miner's Law! Courts were Americo-Mexican, Military-Civil, and Vigilante more than anything else." At last the people of the state took matters into their own hands and called a convention to meet at San Jose, on December 11, 1848. Denouncing the "Squatter Regime," Gov. Bennett Riley, who had succeeded Persifor Smith as military governor, called the first constitutional convention, at Monterey, August 1, 1849. Miguel de Pedrorena and Henry Hill were delegates from San Diego. A constitution was formed at this convention, state boundaries were set, and Peter H. Burnett, pioneer Democrat, was elected the first governor. A year later, on September 9, 1850, President Fillmore signed the bill which admitted California into the Union.

San Diego headed the list of 27 counties created by the new government. The eastern boundary was the present Arizona state line, and the area included the present San Diego County, Imperial County, all, save a narrow western strip, of the present Riverside and San Bernardino Counties, and the eastern half of Inyo County. In 1851, it was cut to an area which included the present San Diego, Imperial, and most of Riverside Counties.

In 1850, Old Town and La Playa were rivals as a site for the San Diego of the future. Citizens of the district bought land in both places and vied with each other in predicting which would be of most importance. Property of the county was valued in that year at slightly over a half-million dollars, three-fourths of it being within the city itself. The city of San Diego was incorporated, and the first election held. The city fathers passed an ordinance fixing the salaries of city officials at a total of $6,800 per annum, but after the veto of the mayor, Joshua Bean, they passed a new ordinance appropriating $2,400 for salaries. But evidently the treasury of $10,610 was too good to be left idle. On October 14, the council appropriated $500 for a ball to honor the United States Coast Survey, and a few days later, $300 for a ball to honor the admission of California into the Union.

In the meanwhile, a movement to start a new San Diego was afoot. Lieutenant Gray, of the Boundary Survey, had seen the sandy shelf of land where modern downtown San Diego is situated, and decided that it was an ideal place for a town. He convinced several others, including William Heath Davis, Miguel de Pedrorena, José Antonio Aguirre, and William C. Ferrell, and together they formed a company. One hundred and sixty acres of city land were purchased for $2,304, bounded by the present Broadway, Front Street, and the harbor. Around a plaza, Pantoja Park, the new city was laid out. Davis bought a shipload of portable houses, lumber, and bricks in San Francisco, which he shipped to San Diego. The first house built in the new subdivision was his own. The United States Government built a military base and barracks in the new town, and here the first school was opened. In 1851, John Judson Ames, an itinerant journalist, landed in New Town and started publishing the San Diego *Herald,* 12 days later than the Los Angeles *Star,* the earliest paper in southern California. The new settlement depended upon burros and wagons to supply drinking water, which was carried from the San Diego River, 3 miles to the north. Ten years later the soldiers dug a well, but by that time the town had ceased to exist as a town, only the barracks and governmental depot remaining. With the outbreak of the Civil War, the troops were gradually withdrawn, and New Town, or "Davis' Folly" as it was derisively called, was abandoned. The businessmen moved back to Old Town, and in 1853, Ames took the *Herald* to Old Town. There it remained until 1860, when it ceased publication.

The Americans who had drifted into San Diego during the 1840's and 1850's intermarried with the Spanish and Mexican families, and it was not long before the government was almost entirely in the hands of these pioneers. The town was infested with rowdies, adventurers, and drifters who ran "hog-wild" with little official correction. True, the *Herald* frequently turned its editorial eye upon the scene, and grew sarcastic about the lack of civic pride in law enforcement, but it was many years before any corrective measures were taken. The Indians were a problem in themselves, and little wonder, for every other house was a saloon, where the Indians could get liquor freely. Killings were frequent. The *Herald* commented on one escapade: "A lot of greasers had a *baile*

38

(Sp., *ball*) the other evening, and as that was not enough for one night, they turned to and stoned a poor Indian, belonging to Mrs. Marron, until he quietly laid down and died. This is considered fine sport, and as our magistrates don't trouble about such little matters, it will probably be repeated on the next occasion, with perhaps slight variations."

Recognizing the need of a good jail, for the old adobe in the center of the plaza which had been used for that purpose had long since outlived its usefulness, the city fathers opened bids for a new one, to be built of stone. The Israel brothers bid low at $3,000, but the contract was awarded to Agostin Haraszthy for $5,000. His father, Charles Haraszthy, was a member of the common council. Within a few months, after laying a part of the cobblestone walls in a mortar without cement, rain damaged the uncompleted building. Haraszthy complained that he would be unable to finish it without a further allotment. He was granted another $2,000. The whole graft would have been nothing out of the ordinary, if the city had received any satisfaction from its finished jail, but it is reported that one of the first prisoners managed to dig his way out with a pocketknife.

The last Indian trouble of any great importance, the Garra uprising, occurred in November of 1851. Antonio Garra, a chief of the Cupeño Indians of Warner Hot Springs, was incited by Bill Marshall, a white trader, to revolt. Garra himself was an honorable man, rather well educated, who believed in his cause. He wished to free the Indians of California and again establish independence for his people. The Warner Ranch was attacked and several persons were killed. The ringleaders of the uprising were captured, and on January 10, 1852, were executed.

In 1852 the city charter was repealed, and the government vested in a board of trustees. The treasury's $10,610 was depleted; the city had issued scrip, and the city fathers found this move was the safest way out of a bad predicament. City administration had been lax, the public officials being frequently too busy with their own business to take care of civic affairs. In 1852, Philip Crosthwaite, the county clerk and recorder, was deputized to hold at one time the offices of all the other county officials, because they were away at a *fiesta*. Outlawry was so open that a law was passed inflicting the death penalty, at the discretion of the jury, for any theft above the value of $50. A rowdy character, one Yankee Jim Robinson, was hanged under this law for stealing a rowboat. Justice was administered more often by inspiration than by code. It is recorded of Charles Haraszthy, while justice of the peace, that he always entered judgment against the party who had money or property. In the case of Couts vs. Morales, he entered judgment against Couts for 25 cents, though it should have been against Morales. Couts swore he wouldn't pay, and Haraszthy was in something of a quandary. When it was suggested that he enter the judgment against the right man, Morales, he replied, "Vell, but dis man, he got no moneys. Ve must gif de shudgment to de man vat gifts us de pizness!"

In 1853, a remarkable man arrived in Old Town. He was Lt. George Horatio Derby, sent by the Government to build a dike across the river flats to turn the San Diego River into Mission Bay. During his 2 years in Old Town he created an impression which remained for many years. In the fall of 1853, while Editor Ames was in San Francisco, Derby was left in charge of the *Herald*. For 6 weeks he edited the paper under the pen name of *John Phoenix*. He turned it topsy-turvy with his wit, changing the editorial political policy and in one issue satirizing the growing interest in illustrated newspapers by issuing a "Phoenix Illustrated Edition." In 1855, Ames, while in the East, issued a volume of Derby's writings, *Phoenixiana,* and 10 years later, posthumously, a second volume appeared: *The Squibob Papers,* which took its title from another of Derby's pen names, John Q. Squibob. In 1855, Derby was sole owner of the *Herald,* and made a contract with William H. Noyes, by which the latter edited the paper, receiving two-thirds of the returns. After that year, Derby was transferred to other parts of the country.

During the 1850's the first major attempt was made to bring a railroad to San Diego. The San Diego & Gila Railroad project created intense excitement for many years, but finally died out completely in the early 1870's. Transportation was mainly by stage. The Giddings and Woods pack train line started service between San Diego and San Antonio, Texas, on August 9, 1857. In the following year the Butterfield Stages were first operated and continued running until the outbreak of the Civil War. After 1865, the Capron line operated between San Diego and Los Angeles, and in 1867, through the influence of Major Ben Truman, postal agent for California, San Diego became a secondary terminal for the El Paso route.

With the arrival of Alonzo Erastus Horton on April 15, 1867, Old Town, and all that it represented in Spanish and Mexican heritage, was given its deathblow, though at the time no one would have pictured the sturdy, tight-lipped little Yankee as an angel of doom. Horton was shrewd. He saw at a glance that if San Diego was to grow into an important seaport city, it must be moved to the present downtown site. Horton was a go-getter, in its most modern sense. Learning that the city fathers were continuing in office illegally to save the expense of an election, Horton himself put up the money. He picked his own candidates, had them elected, and then bought at auction the city lands he wanted. The 1,000 acres which he bought cost him about 21 cents an acre. It was a whirlwind affair. Within a few weeks he had platted the new town and was advertising in the San Francisco papers. At the foot of Fifth Avenue he built a wharf costing $45,000, and within a short time several houses were built and a hotel was opened. Horton, a "Black Republican," announced that only Republicans would receive work from his jobs, though San Diego was a stronghold of the Democrats. The Republican majority quite naturally grew by leaps and bounds.

The 226 blocks of Horton's Addition, as the town was called, sold so swiftly that Horton often complained that he became tired of handling so much money. He donated land to churches, gave the site for a courthouse, and even offered property free to individuals who would immediately erect houses upon it.

San Diego became real estate mad. People lived in tents on their lots until they could clear away the brush and cactus. More frequently they sold out at fancy prices before they could settle on the land. Buyers bought from maps without inspecting the purchase, and in turn sold to other speculators, sight unseen. Other subdivisions developed. Sherman's Addition, east of Fifteenth Street, opened in 1868, and although it was mainly a section of ravines and sand hills, sold rapidly.

The first official act to establish a city park occurred on February 15, 1868. The city fathers inspected 160 acres of waste mesa land, north of Horton's Addition, and the very bleakness of the land made them generous. Instead of the 160 acres originally inspected, they put aside 1,400 acres for a park, to be kept perpetually for that purpose. Luckily for the modern city, this act was ratified by the State legislature, because even this tract came under the rapacious eyes of the land sharks within a few years, and only the law of the land kept the park intact.

Between 1860, the year the *Herald* ceased publication, and 1868, San Diego had no newspaper of its own. On October 10, 1868, the San Diego *Union* started publication in Old Town, and in 1870 moved to Horton's Addition. Old Town was fighting a losing battle. One by one the merchants moved to the new town, officially called South San Diego. A move was started to transfer the county seat to Horton's town, which was opposed bitterly by the Old Town property owners. On April 3, 1871, with a secrecy which public excitement demanded, the records were bundled into a wagon and moved to a temporary courthouse in New Town. Old Town gave up the struggle. It became officially North San Diego after that. When a fire swept the south side of the plaza, in 1872, many of the business houses were destroyed, and Old Town's importance as a community was ended.

Gold was discovered in the Julian area in February of 1870, and this did much to bring people to the county. By 1873 so many people were settled in Julian and Banner that a serious attempt was made to transfer the county seat to Julian. This effort failed. In the 18 years of mining activity it is estimated that more than 15 million dollars' worth of gold was removed from the district.

Horton startled the city in 1870 by building a hotel on the present site of the U. S. Grant Hotel. The business center at that time was at Fifth Avenue and Market Street. It was madness, so everyone said, for him to move so far out of the center of things. But Horton was shrewd enough to see that Broadway was to become the main artery of the town. The Horton House, which opened on October 10, 1870, was a miracle of its day, with one hundred rooms, and a "Ladies' Parlor" the only one of its kind south of San Francisco. The whole job had cost $150,000. Awe-stricken citizens and travelers admired its black walnut furniture and its marble-topped washstands.

The great "Tom Scott Boom" started in 1872. The Kimball brothers, founders of National City, negotiated with Tom Scott, a railroad magnate, to make San Diego and National City the terminal for a transcontinental railroad. The city's population rose to four thousand. Lots changed hands as often as five times a day, each sale boosting the original price by hundreds of dollars. When the pro-

41

posed Texas & Pacific Railroad failed to materialize, the bubble broke, and a period of despondency and business inactivity followed.

The San Diego *Sun,* now a Scripps-Howard paper, was first issued on July 19, 1881.

Not until 1885 did the railroad finally arrive, and then it was a branch of the Santa Fe system. A second boom followed. Insane real estate speculation swept the citizens off their feet, and it was evident that they had learned nothing from the previous experience. Building activities were mushroomlike, and the ornate "gingerbread" style of that period spread over the town like a lacework veneer.

By 1887 it is estimated that the population had risen to forty thousand, the crest of the boom. Houses were built, wharves constructed, and every type of business house arose where only brush and lizards had been seen a few months before. Board sidewalks and sand were everywhere, and, as one pioneer recorded, "the sand was full of fleas." The boom ended as suddenly as it started. By 1890 there were barely seventeen thousand people in the city. The community settled down to a slow, steady increase, more consistent with healthy growth, and in the long run more beneficial. But during the boom several progressive things had come to the city. The first train from the East arrived on November 21, 1885; the first electric lights and horse cars began operation in 1886; the first electric streetcar line, the third in the world, started in 1887; and in 1888 the first modern dam, that on the Sweetwater River, was completed. Gas and telephone services had been established in 1881 and 1882.

Between 1890 and 1910, the city's growth was due mainly to individuals like the Spreckels brothers. John D. Spreckels came to San Diego from San Francisco, and saw possibilities in the new town. He and his brother bought and controlled large holdings. They purchased the entire property of the Coronado Beach Company, which had opened the Hotel del Coronado in February of 1888, and the present city of Coronado is the result of their interest in the area. The confidence and investments of John D. Spreckels did much to revive financial and civic morale, so that, when the panic of 1893 swept the country, San Diego was little affected. Besides it had already had its share of economic depression.

In 1895, 7 years after the collapse of the "Great Boom," San Diego had 30 churches, 6 banks, 82 attorneys, and 9 drygoods stores. The *Evening Tribune* started publication in December of 1895, and in 1901 it was purchased by the Spreckels interests and added to the San Diego *Union,* which they already owned. Both papers are still in existence.

With the turn of the century, San Diego's growth passed its critical period. Steadily, since then, the population has increased, almost doubling itself every 10 years. (See table, p. 49.) Among the factors which helped to stabilize local values was the construction of the San Diego & Arizona Eastern Railroad, begun in 1908 and completed in 1919. Funds were appropriated by the Government in 1907 to build the United States Naval Coaling Station, on Point Loma, and this was the entering wedge for an ever increasing expenditure for military purposes. In 1907 San Diego County was made smaller by the withdrawal of the present Imperial County. In 1909 plans were begun for the Panama-California

HORTON HOUSE, ON THE SITE OF PRESENT U. S. GRANT HOTEL,
PLAZA IN FOREGROUND *(Fitch Studio photograph)*

FIFTH AVENUE IN THE 80's, LOOKING
NORTH *(Averett photograph)*

Exposition, which opened in 1915. San Diego was presented to the millions of visitors as a desirable residential town and place for retirement. John Nolen, internationally known city planner, was brought to San Diego in 1907 and drew up the Nolen Plan for civic improvement, which, with necessary modifications, is being followed in all major civic developments.

The panic of 1907-1908 was not felt noticeably in San Diego, and though a 6 months' legal holiday was declared in the state, the city was not forced to issue scrip.

San Diego's reputation as an ideal area for aviation development is of long standing. On January 26, 1911, Glenn Curtiss made his famous hydroplane test flight from North Island and remained aloft for 1 minute 24 seconds. In 1927, Charles Lindbergh supervised the construction of his ship, *The Spirit of St. Louis,* in San Diego, and started from here for the east coast, before taking off for Paris. The recent growth of aviation production plants has made San Diego one of the major centers for this industry.

San Diego's real economic and social development has occurred since the exposition of 1915, augmented by that of 1935-36. It is today securely established as an important naval center and looks forward to an almost unlimited development in the industrial fields.

ECONOMIC

THE DEVELOPMENT OF SAN DIEGO

Agriculture during the first century of San Diego's history was for a time the only local industry, and throughout that period was dominant in the general economy. Gradually other industrial activities developed, beginning with the hide and tallow trade and later including the short-lived whaling industry, and culminating in the fishing industry which is now of considerable importance. In the 1880's the first steps were taken to conserve and pipe to the city the abundant back country water supply. From that time diversified industrial establishments began to appear, their number and size generally restricted by the supply of water. As the numerous watersheds in the county were developed, San Diego assumed more importance as an industrial center. Today (1937) there are 335 factories of all types, the largest of which is the Consolidated Aircraft Corporation, employing more than three thousand workers.

The padres were the first men to develop the resources of this area. For the first quarter century after their arrival, they concentrated on the production of foodstuffs, but ill luck attended most of the early plantings. The first acreage was washed out by a river flood; the second, because of an attempt to avoid the fate of the first, was planted too far away from water, and it, too, failed. The third attempt, 10 miles up the river, succeeded, and 20 bushels of wheat were harvested. By 1790, 1,500 bushels were being harvested annually. Olives, pears, and pomegranates were planted at an early date, and olive production became an important portion of the economy of the missions. The building of a dam in the first quarter of the nineteenth century and laying of tile conduits, greatly aided the padres in making tillable soil of otherwise arid land. This constituted the first attempt by white men at systematic irrigation in California.

The padres encouraged the Indians to hunt for fur-bearing animals, particularly the sea otter, then plentiful along the harbor shore; and with the pelts, trade was established between the missions and the Spanish merchant ships that came up the coast from Mexico and South America.

For a century after the founding of San Diego in 1769, cattle raising was the most important industry throughout the state. By 1830 the few animals which had been brought in with the several expeditions had increased to fifteen thousand head of cattle, twenty thousand sheep, and many thousands of hogs. The cattle were wastefully slaughtered, because the parts that were of value to the trading ships were the hides and tallow. A few choice parts of the meat were saved for food, but the balance of the carcass was left on the ground to rot. Point Loma, the site of the hide houses, was an odorous area in the early days, if accounts of pioneers may be credited. The hide and tallow trade reached its peak between 1821 and 1845; and Dana's *Two Years Before the Mast* describes the hide trade at its best in 1835. Prior to 1820, all trade with California was a Spanish government monopoly, and there were frequent clashes between the authorities and the foreign ships, usually Yankee, that attempted to smuggle goods from the country. The pioneer hide ship was the *Sachem* of Boston, which arrived on the California coast in 1822.

Whales were a common sight in and around San Diego harbor in the early days, and by 1853 whaling began to assume economic importance. Two companies were operating from Ballast Point on Point Loma by 1863, and it was a favorite sport for the townspeople to watch from the lighthouse grounds. (See *Tour* 2.) There were times when it was unsafe to cross the bay in a rowboat because of the number of whales, 40 having been reported as visible at one time. Because of the increase in shipping and the ruthless hunting, whales deserted this area, and the whale-oil industry died.

San Diego's real growth began after 1872, which local historians call the "year of awakening." In that year the town's business was mainly in Horton's Addition, though a few stubborn pioneers refused to desert Old Town. At that time there were 2 commission houses, 2 wholesale liquor houses, 2 millinery stores, 7 hotels, 3 fancy goods stores, 3 lumber yards, 2 furniture stores, 4 drug stores, 2 tinware stores, 2 book stores, 5 livery stables, 2 fruit stores, 1 bank, and 23 saloons, which the San Diego *World* recommended with the comment that "they dispense an excellent article of whiskey." One boot and shoe shop, 1 sash and building furnisher, 2 Chinese stores, 2 jewelry stores, 4 restaurants, 2 breweries, 1 foundry, 20 general merchandise stores, and 2 steam planing mills complete the business index for the period. In January of 1870 the San Diego Chamber of Commerce was organized; and according to the *Weekly Bulletin* of that month, "the adaptability of cotton, to this section, is attracting attention." Shortly before this date, the same paper felt called upon to comment editorially upon certain business needs. "Our City is in need of a good laundry, and the first one that starts will command a large custom. There is but one shoemaker in the city, when a half a dozen more could have all they could do."

In 1870 a telegraph line was constructed, which gave San Diego a news contact with the world. In the early 1880's the first gas company was organized and began operation. In 1882 the San Diego Telephone Company began operation with 13 subscribers. Electricity came in 1886, and tall street lights, three and four times the height of present-day lamps, were a characteristic of early San Diego street scenes.

From the beginning it was apparent that water development held the key to the city's growth. There existed an abundance of water in the numerous back country watersheds, and practically none in the city proper. To insure San Diego's expansion, development of these watersheds was an urgent necessity. Only water conservation, through construction of dams and reservoirs, could insure an adequate supply for irrigation, industry, and home consumption. When Horton's Addition was first opened, water was carried by wagon from the San Diego River, and marketed at 25 cents a pail. Later a few independent wells were dug, that, together with the river water, sufficed for a time. In 1873 the San Diego Water Company struck an artesian flow near Balboa Park that supplied two reservoirs with 54,000 gallons of water an hour. In 1885, the San Diego Flume Company started the first major attempt to pipe

TRAINLOADS OF LAND SPECULATORS WERE TYPICAL
OF THE BOOM PERIODS *(Averett photograph)*

GLENN CURTISS AND HIS FIRST HYDROPLANE MADE
HISTORY IN 1911 *(Fitch Studio photograph)*

water to the city from a distance. The flood water of the Cuyamaca Mountains area was impounded behind a clay and concrete embankment. Cuyamaca Lake still exists, and the original dam is in use, though its height has been increased. The overflow from this dam followed the regular riverbed to a point 35 miles from the mouth of the San Diego River, and from that point a wooden flume transported the water to the city's edge, and underground pipes delivered it from that point into the main part of town. On February 22, 1889, the flume was opened with a mammoth celebration. After a parade more than a mile long, a hydrant was turned on and a stream of water shot 125 feet into the air, to the intense admiration of the citizenry. Actually the Cuyamaca water, forcing itself slowly through the air-bound pipes, was still 13 miles from the city, and did not reach the delivery point for 3 weeks. But the people did not know this. Rather than disappoint the holiday makers, and also to save the company's face, the rival San Diego Water Company turned its own water into the pipes. No doubt officials of this company enjoyed the crowd's enthusiastic praise of "the excellent taste of the new water."

A year after the San Diego Flume Company was initiated, the Sweetwater Dam was projected. For its time this dam was an engineering triumph and civil engineers the world over came to give it careful study. It now has a storage capacity of more than 10 billion gallons, and cost approximately one-half million dollars.

In March of 1886 the Otay Water Company was formed to develop the Otay watershed. Later this company combined with others in the Southern California Mountain Water Company which built the Upper and Lower Otay and Morena Dams. In 1906, this company entered into a contract with the city to deliver a maximum of nearly 8 million gallons of water daily at a stipulated low price for a period of 10 years. This was the first adequate supply of mountain water to become accessible. By 1901 the city had begun to develop its own water system by purchasing the San Diego Water Company, to which it added, in 1913, the facilities of the Southern California Mountain Water Company. The San Dieguito Mutual Water Company, which in 1918 had built Hodges Dam and reservoir near Escondido, was leased by the city in 1925, with an option to purchase, and this reservoir furnished an adequate supply for La Jolla and other communities in that area. In 1923 the city completed Barrett Dam; El Capitan Dam and Reservoir, the largest hydraulic fill, rock embankment in the world, was completed in 1935.

The first effort to obtain railroad transportation, made in the 1850's, proved a fiasco, and not until 1885 did the first train come through. To make this possible, San Diego and National City each provided a subsidy of 3 million dollars, and additional property to the value of 7 million dollars, which were given to the Santa Fe Railroad to connect San Diego with the transcontinental lines. This was about twice as much as the line from San Diego to Barstow actually cost. In return for this subsidy, the donors received no shares of railroad stock, and had to accept the promise of railroad executives that the terminal would remain in National City. Despite this promise, the Santa Fe moved its terminal shops to San Bernardino after a few years, and San Diego was left with a branch line and infrequent service. But with the railroad came an increase in business and real estate activity. The great boom period of 1886 to 1888 followed, and population figures jumped from about five thousand to more than forty thousand. (See table below.) In 1886 the number of business firms and professional men in town was 340, but a year later it was 957. City property jumped from an evaluation of $4,-582,213 to $13,182,171 in the same period. Speculation was the order of the day, and property values skyrocketed as much as a thousand percent in a single day. Predictions were indulged in, freely. San Diego was to become the metropolis of the west coast. Hordes of speculators, gamblers, promoters, and adventurers of every type flooded the city, attracted by the prospect of easy money. In 1888 the boom collapsed. Property values fell tremendously, and many families were left destitute. Ten thousand persons departed the city within a few months. Readjustment followed slowly, yet after a few years the city settled down to a slow, even tempo of expansion and development, which was to prove the proper course. Settlers who had weathered the boom era, and the newcomers who came because of the real merits of the area, were firm boosters, and it was this class which ultimately made the city what it is.

Since 1900, San Diego has doubled its population every 10 years, as the following figures for each decade show, until today it ranks the fourth city in size in California.

1850	650	1890	16,156
1860	731	1900	17,700
1870	2,300	1910	39,578
1880	2,637	1920	74,683
1884	5,000 (est.)	1924	110,000 (est.)
1886	40,000 (est.)	1930	147,897
1888	35,000 (est.)	1937	183,800 (est.)

In 1906 the San Diego & Arizona Railroad Company was organized —John D. Spreckels, president—and San Diego's dream of a direct line to the East was revived. The driving of a golden spike in the last tie on November 15, 1919, was the climax of 13 years of hopeful effort.

Although there are 335 factories in San Diego, predominantly small manufacturing establishments, it cannot properly be termed an industrial city, as compared with San Francisco, Seattle, or Los Angeles. The percentage of industrial workers is considerably less than that of the northern cities. San Diego's smokeless sky testifies to the almost complete absence of typical large-scale industries. From the standpoint of local revenue, this is compensated by the presence of retired midwestern farmers, civil service pensioners, and retired army and navy personnel. In this connection it is interesting to note that approximately 10 percent of the retired navy officers in the United States have chosen San Diego as their home.

Some local businessmen insist that a portion of the population for years has resisted all attempts to industrialize the city. This conflict has delayed the construction of adequate highways and railroad lines at the critical period when industry was flocking to the west coast, with the result that business which could have been induced to locate here was forced to go elsewhere. When Imperial Valley cotton production was at its peak, in 1917 and 1918, leading cotton brokers investigated the possibility of improving the transportation lines from Imperial Valley to San

Diego, because San Diego harbor was considered a better shipping point than Los Angeles harbor, but this move failed, because of the antipathy of the conservative portion of the residents. Before Los Angeles improved its harbor facilities, cargoes for that city were received in San Diego harbor and shipped by rail to the northern city. But as Los Angeles improved San Pedro harbor, San Diego lost business. When the need for improved transportation was realized, the major industries had already settled elsewhere.

The principal basic sources of the city's income are: factories, including the fishing industry, with an annual payroll of 20 million dollars; Navy, Marine, and Government personnel of twenty-seven thousand with an annual payroll of 24 million dollars; and retired business men and farmers who contribute an incalculable sum to the city's income.

Since the whaling days, fishing has been identified with San Diego's industrial life. At present three categories—deep-sea fishing, fresh market fishing, and canning—employ more than four thousand men and women, with annual production valued at more than 10 million dollars. Market fishing alone brings in about three-quarters of a million dollars annually.

Of the several lumber companies, one is widely known because each year the largest log rafts in the world are assembled in the great timber lands of the Northwest and towed to the plant's San Diego mills. Other manufactured products include agar, a seaweed product; oil-burning stoves; numerous candy preparations, one factory producing 750,000 pounds annually; and an onyx and marble novelties company, unique of its kind. In all more than 150 articles of commerce are manufactured in the city and county of San Diego.

A recent census conducted by the Chamber of Commerce indicates that 60,897 of the estimated city population of one hundred and eighty thousand are gainfully employed. The official government census figure of 1930 revealed that forty-eight thousand were gainfully employed of a population of 147,897 persons.

Year in and year out, regardless of the condition of business and industry, the military and governmental pay roll sustains a considerable portion of the retail merchandising establishments. This economic cushion has kept San Diego from feeling the full effects of depression periods. The presence of this force of twenty-seven thousand men also tends to stabilize rents, as 60 percent of these men live ashore and 40 percent are married. Although ships are constantly being transferred to other bases and lengthy maneuvers are frequently held, it is estimated that ten thousand sailors and marines is the minimum number in the city at any time.

Local Works Progress Administration projects are emergency enterprises, but the WPA has undertaken at least five major projects in recent years—the Civic Center, the County Fair buildings, the State College Stadium, the enlargement of Lindbergh Field, and additions to the San Diego Zoo, besides numerous important road projects. Reconditioning of schools, road work, harbor work, pest control, and general construction are a few of the big projects for men. Women are given work in sewing projects, the care of children, visual education projects, and library and clerical work. In 1936 relief jobs employed more than six thousand

SWEETWATER DAM, AN ENGINEERING FEAT
OF THE 80's *(Averett photograph)*

LINDBERGH FIELD, THE MUNICIPAL
AIRPORT *(Sensor Studios photograph)*

persons and added approximately four hundred and fifty thousand dollars monthly to the city's income.

Farming, dairying, and poultry and stock raising are carried on extensively in the 4,125 square miles of San Diego County lying outside the city limits, with a total yearly output valued in excess of 15 million dollars. Agricultural production alone reaches 10 million dollars a year. Principal crops produced, largely for export, are lemons, oranges, limes, grapefruit, avocados, celery, grapes, honey, bulbs, and flowers. In the frostless areas of the county many tropical and subtropical fruits are grown, such as mangoes, passion fruit, bananas, pineapples, dates, guavas, pomegranates, figs, and olives. The growing of avocados is so successful that more than 8,000 acres are planted to this fruit. More than 5,000 acres in lemon orchards are expected to produce a yield this year (1937) valued at almost 2 million dollars. Approximately 1,115 acres are planted to celery with an annual production value of one million dollars.

While the tendency is toward an industrial San Diego, at the present time (1937) the city is distinctly a merchandising center, since this type of business dominates the local economic scene. There are more than four thousand retail stores in San Diego, with total annual sales of approximately 65 million dollars. Many chain retail concerns maintain large branch stores. It is estimated that the number of retail stores in relationship to the population is considerably higher than in the average city, probably due to the number of wealthy individuals and retired pensioners living here.

Labor conditions in San Diego city and county reflect the national trend toward increased union membership. The present conflict between craft and industrial unions is likewise reflected here with both the American Federation of Labor and the Committee for Industrial Organization vigorously campaigning for domination of the local labor scene. The attitude of employers toward this development seems to vary, although generally union organization is resented and opposed. In most instances, however, this opposition is reconciled before strikes and labor disturbances can occur, for San Diego is remarkably free from such conflicts. With the development of a score of new unions in the city in the past 2 years, including organizations in every important local industry, San Diego can no longer be classified as "open shop." Wages and working conditions compare favorably with other southern California counties. Lowest wages paid are for agricultural and orchard work, where the scale for unskilled labor varies from 25 to 30 cents an hour. Many agricultural workers, mostly Mexicans, are members of the United Cannery, Agricultural, Packing, and Allied Workers of America, which seeks each year to win contracts from growers governing wages and working conditions. One of the most powerful labor unions in the city proper is the Aircraft union, whose union contract provides for wages ranging from 50 cents to $1.25 an hour, and for regulation of working conditions, including protection of the seniority rights of workers and recognition of the shop steward system, which functions to settle grievances amicably. Deep-sea, purse-seine, and market fishermen, and cannery workers recently were organized into unions; and the retail clerks' and culinary unions have attained large memberships. Sixteen building trades unions are federated in the Building Trades Council, and represent approximately half of the workers in the building industry. Wages for this group range from 62½ cents an hour for building construction laborers, to $2 an hour for the "modelers," who are the sculptors of building friezes. Many crafts receive $1.25 an hour, including the electricians, plumbers, plasterers, and brick masons. Carpenters receive $1 an hour.

The remainder of San Diego's 45 labor unions are found in miscellaneous trades, such as motion-picture houses, machine shops, breweries, newspapers, job printing shops, trucking concerns, meat markets and grocery stores, laundries, bakeries, clothing shops, hotels, and on the docks, where the stevedores are represented by the powerful International Longshoremen's and Warehousemen's Union. Most of the firemen, postal employees, and county employees belong to labor unions, although the constitutions of their unions prohibit strikes against their employers.

San Diego is provided with every variety of modern transportation— rail, water, trucking, bus, and air. The first three groups receive almost equal patronage in freight shipments in and out of the city, although business leaders emphasize the importance of shipping by water to assist in developing the harbor. Regular freighters call at the port at frequent intervals, and many tramp freighters dock here. Shipping by air express is gaining in favor, and one company reports an average air express shipment of 106 pounds a month, with patronage growing.

Agricultural communities around San Diego are served with railroad spur lines, and trucking concerns maintain daily schedules to these points.

Highways are well developed in San Diego city and county. The county has constructed and maintains 2,300 miles of improved and unimproved roads outside of the city; the state maintains 600 miles of roads within the county; and the city has built and continues to maintain within its geographical limits 1,025 miles of road, 562 of which are paved. (For detailed information on transportation see *General Information*.)

From humble beginnings a half century ago, public utilities have assumed an amazing importance in the city's economy. Water distribution, with the exception of bottled spring waters, is a public enterprise; a private corporation furnishes the city with gas and electricity. Utility rates are considerably higher than in other cities of like size.

To estimate the future growth of San Diego, it is necessary to take cognizance of the fact that resistance to industrial development has been broken, and the desire to bring new industry to the city seems unanimous. And here again water is an important factor. The city still has but a limited water supply and a present income barely sufficient to carry the financial costs of the city water system. It is generally conceded that a lower water rate would result in the locating here of various industries requiring large water consumption and in the planting of acreage now idle but possible to irrigate. The present water supply is believed sufficient to support a population of two hundred and twenty thousand, and the full development of local water resources would support a population of four hundred thousand. If necessary, enough water could be obtained from the Colorado River to support a population of one and one-half millions and provide an ample supply for irrigation.

SOCIAL AND CULTURAL

Because of its varied background and constantly changing social surface, San Diego has never developed a homogeneous social and cultural pattern. In the slightly more than a century and a half of its existence, two distinct racial groups have left their impression upon the area. The first group, the Spanish, dominated until about 1850, replacing almost completely the rudimentary Indian culture of the California coastal region. So completely, in fact, were the Indians subjugated and reoriented on the cultural plane, that at the present time few traces remain of their folkways and to all intents and purposes they are a disintegrated remnant of the Mexican colonial culture. Spanish manners and customs that were superimposed upon Mexico during the Conquest deviated in a short time from their European source, and, transplanted two centuries later to the pioneer outpost of California, additional modifications occurred. The settlers felt this distinction and called themselves *Californios* to differentiate themselves from the *Mexicanos*. Intermarriage between these pioneers and the Indians (a practice sanctioned by the Spanish government for the better subjugation of a province), coupled with the relative isolation of the district, fostered a spirit of independence among the provincials and made them more sharply aware of the new and subtle differences between themselves and the mother country.

After 1810, Americans came to the Pacific coast in ever-increasing numbers, attracted either by commercial potentialities or by the sheer incentive of adventure. Mexico officially frowned upon the presence of foreigners in California; but the hardy and shrewd Yankees, not to be balked in their intention to harvest this rich field, took out naturalization papers and married into the pioneer families. That such marriages brought large dowries to the Americans was frequently incentive enough for renouncing allegiance to the United States. Henry Delano Fitch, a New England sea captain, was certainly such a commercial adventurer. He arrived in California in the latter part of the 1820's, and his romance and elopement with Josefa Carrillo, of San Diego, is typical of what was happening in the whole territory. After his naturalization, and conversion to the Catholic faith, a necessary procedure, he emerged as Enrique Domingo Fitch, Californian; yet as late as 1840 he petitioned the Governor to allow him a secretary, in his capacity of Justice of the Peace, because—so little did the Spanish setting modify the American type—"he does not understand Spanish."

The Californians were an easygoing people, fond of entertainment, and especially inclined to any activity which involved the whole community. The settlements of California were small, rarely more than a few hundred people, and the heads of families were usually members of the local garrisons. Surrounding the towns and *presidios* were farm tracts, or *ranchos*, where the families spent much of their time. Cattle raising was the most important factor in their economic life, and community interests and social activities evolved naturally from this environment.

54

BUILDING SAN DIEGO BY CHARLES REIFFEL
(*Federal Art Project photograph*)

The rodeo—which is still held to demonstrate the cowboy's prowess—
was a diversion of these people. Bullfights were fairly common, and to
this sport was sometimes added that of pitting bears against bulls in the
arena. Bears were not only dangerous but a nuisance to the cattle
ranchers because of their slaughter of stock.

The majority of social events, however, revolved naturally around
the Catholic church. Holidays, births, marriages, and even deaths were
subjects for entertainment. To the puritanically-minded New Englander
many of the California customs were surprising if not shocking. Robinson, in his *Life in California,* written about his experiences here in the
1820's, noted particularly the carefree way in which even funerals were
conducted. On one occasion he visited an American friend (who had
married into a Spanish family), and he received the impression that a
fiesta was in progress. Actually, the man had lost a daughter. The
funeral procession was gay and colorful, with children running and
playing beside the coffin, alternating with each other in carrying it.

After 1850, Spanish culture faded into insignificance. Newcomers
poured into the territory by thousands, in search of gold, and were
little concerned with any culture. Many amassed fortunes in the mines,
but landsharks also grew wealthy from the manipulation of the great
ranchos, which they acquired through the use of legal but frequently
shady methods. Few of the native Californians ever learned the American way of doing things, and the American system of law, particularly,
was beyond their comprehension. The Spanish methods had been an
outgrowth of honesty and the individual's integrity; the American seemed

to many of them to have sprung from thin scruples and an uncanny awareness of legal loopholes. One *rancho* in the San Diego area was acquired by a ruse which proved entirely legal at the time. A landshark, desiring a particular piece of ground, called upon the Spanish lady who owned it, accompanied by two assistants. The owner knew no English, but one of the assistants, a Californian known to her, acted as go-between. They told her that a government census was being taken, and would she give them certain information about the *rancho*? She complied with the request and at the end of the interview was asked to sign a paper. Only a formality, she was assured; the government wanted to have each statement legal. She signed, and the assistants witnessed the transaction. She was then handed a twenty-dollar gold piece. The government, they assured her, did not like to encroach upon the valuable time of individuals. They always paid for such services. A few days later the woman found that she had sold her ranch for $20, and had signed the deed before witnesses. She had no witnesses, so there was no redress. In such ways were many Californians expropriated and many American fortunes acquired.

With the founding of New San Diego, in 1867, Alonzo Horton started a distinctly American town. His was the new spirit, the busy, rushing American urge to build and speculate. California was now American, and the spoils went to the astute. The new town soon filled with middle-class mercantile establishments and land speculators. Out in Old Town the business concerns fought hard against the inevitable transfer of interest to Horton's Addition, but by 1870 it was evident to all but a few die-hards that the old days were finished.

The rising population of the boom years brought a wide variety of racial groups. The last quarter of the nineteenth century witnessed several distinct divisions of society. The Portuguese and Italians were developing the fishing industry; the Government started improving the harbor for naval purposes; and, on the wave of publicity, middle western and eastern farmers and merchants were being given an attractive picture of San Diego as the ideal place for retirement.

Racial minority groups compose about 15 percent of the present population. The largest number of these are the Californians and the Mexicans, the first term being applied to those persons of Spanish descent who are native to the state. The foreign-born Mexicans are principally located in the Logan Heights area, and Old Town is the center for the native-born. The majority of the Mexicans are of recent arrival. Between 1917 and 1930, numbers of migratory unskilled laborers moved their families into California on being promised railroad construction work. The railroads were soon built, and the Mexicans turned to agricultural work, which, being seasonal at best, was not able to absorb the oversupply of labor. Left to their own devices, they turned to day labor, a large number being in demand as cement workers during the building activities of the 1920's. Wives of the workers found employment in the fish canneries or at miscellaneous work away from home.

In their new homes, the Mexicans continued to follow their ancestral cultural patterns. Native games and tales have persisted; and such examples of Mexican wit as revealed in anagrams, sayings, fables, riddles, and *corridos* (Sp., *a story of everyday happenings set to music*) continue a part of their new life. The Mexican is very fond of the devil-story— usually a tall tale of personal experience told impromptu and with childlike realism. The younger generation is breaking away from its racial traditions and appears to be adopting the current American manners and customs. This is true of the youth of nearly all the minority groups. The cultural activities of their elders, insofar as they concern the old national folkways, are separate from the general stream of modern life. In Logan Heights is a social service agency for the Mexicans, the Neighborhood House, which is similar to Hull House of Chicago. Its files list more than five hundred families who receive aid and advice from the agency's staff. A playground in connection offers a safe community center for the younger children. San Diego's Mexican population is probably smaller at present (1937) than in 1930 because many families have returned to Mexico, but it still numbers about five thousand.

Even more segregated are the five thousand Portuguese who reside along the bay side of Point Loma. Fishermen by birth and instinct, they operate the fleet of tuna clippers that supplies San Diego's canneries. This minority group contributes the largest single item to San Diego's income, excepting that derived from governmental activities. Present leaders of the colony are mostly foreign-born, though there has been a Portuguese colony in San Diego for almost a hundred years. The Azores and Madeira Islands have supplied the majority of the fishermen, and the customs of those islands prevail. Many of the women and older folk do not speak English. The only factor in their new life which has taken hold of their imaginations is the motion picture. Their exaggerated delight in this form of entertainment frequently takes them to town, but aside from these excursions they do not mix with the general population. Perhaps this isolation is due in part to the fact that during the fishing season the men are away for 3 and 4 months at a time and rigid racial custom does not encourage mixing in the broader life of the community. As the Portuguese fishermen own their own fleet, there is no great need for learning English, and this indifference is naturally reflected in the home.

The Italian residents, almost as numerous as the Portuguese, are also largely employed in the fishing industry. They have smaller boats and are more occupied with supplying the local markets. They form a rather homogeneous unit in the area north of Broadway along Columbia Street; but they are not so clannish as the Portuguese, and several civic leaders have come from their number.

The Negroes of San Diego, about four thousand five hundred persons, live mainly in the region between K Street and Logan Avenue, with a business center at Thirtieth Street and Imperial Avenue. The working population is mainly engaged in manual labor and domestic service. There are nine Negro churches. The Girl Reserves, an affiliation of the Y.W.C.A., has a membership of one hundred girls. The Creole Palace, an established "hot spot," is a night club that caters to white as well as Negro clientele.

The Oriental population of the city is small. Not more than five hundred Chinese of a once large colony continue to live in the Chinatown

57

area, from Fourth Avenue and Market Street to the waterfront. The Japanese, about one thousand in number, are engaged in fishing and vegetable marketing.

Though the racial minority groups maintain their own club and recreational centers, the balance of the population is no less clannish. Clubs and societies of every-description meet throughout the year, catering to one or another interest of their members. The common bond may be an engrossing interest in the high rate of taxes, in old age pensions, in book reviews, in racial relations, or even in some new and subtle distinction in the methodology of star gazing. Southern California seems to incite its citizens to "joining"; and San Diego, with such a large percentage of retired residents, is particularly active in this respect. Among the more characteristic organizations of southern California are the state societies. These are composed of residents who came originally from another state, and who like to meet others from the old home place. A federation of state societies meets monthly in the Chamber of Commerce Building.

While these types of organization are the most numerous, the city has, for example, a number of professional, semiprofessional, and amateur organizations, which present concerts throughout the year. Oldest of these, the Amphion Club, was founded in 1893 and presents an annual season of nationally known artists. The cost of the season is remarkably reasonable, considering the standard of artists selected. During the current season, 1937-1938, such performers as Yehudi Menuhin, the New English Singers, Josef Hofmann, and the Trudi Shoop Ballet are being presented. The average attendance at Amphion performances is 1,400.

In 1927 the San Diego Symphony Orchestra was founded, under the direction of Nino Marcelli, and since then it has given an annual series of concerts during the summer season in Balboa Park. At present the orchestra performs in the Ford Bowl, an outdoor amphitheater built during the recent world fair. The average nightly attendance is about three thousand. Its programs, as a whole, are indicative of the musical taste of San Diego audiences. Tschaikowsky, Wagner, Rimsky-Korsakoff, Liszt, and Mendelssohn are perennial favorites, and no season seems complete without a hearing of Rimsky-Korsakoff's *Spanish Caprice*. The compositions of Charles Wakefield Cadman, a San Diego composer of more than local note, are also frequently played. Occasional departures are made into the heavier symphonic scores, and a season invariably brings at least one Beethoven symphony.

The Federal Music Projects have satisfied a definite need in the community in the short period of their existence. A resume of the attendance and accomplishments of these organizations, as of June 30, 1937, shows 1,427 performances to a total attendance of 934,404 persons. The opera division has presented *The Mikado, The Gondoliers,* and *Iolanthe* of Gilbert and Sullivan, and performances of *Hansel and Gretel,* the *Geisha Girl,* and *Cavalleria Rusticana.* Chamber music, symphonic performances, band concerts, and radio programs have been given, which demonstrates the wide-spread appeal of these groups. Weekly programs, free to the public, are given by the Navy and Marine Bands, and by Royal A. Brown, organist of the great outdoor organ in Balboa Park.

CORONADO YACHT HARBOR *(Chamber of
Commerce photograph)*

PLAYGROUND OF NEIGHBORHOOD HOUSE, SETTLEMENT HOUSE
IN THE MEXICAN QUARTER *(Federal Art Project photograph)*

In the field of drama San Diego has usually depended on road shows, which toured the country regularly before the advent of motion pictures. As early as 1868 there is record of the appearance of a variety troupe at the local meeting house. Except for the work of the Savoy Players, a stock troupe which existed for a number of years, drama has never gained a permanent footing. Today, except for occasional road shows, the popular productions of the Federal Theater Project, and a few little theater and amateur productions, the city is dependent upon the motion picture for dramatic entertainment. The usual opinion of producers is that San Diego audiences are unresponsive.

In common with other communities having a large percentage of retired and semi-independent residents, San Diego has a great number of artists, writers, musicians, and amateur artisans. The San Diego Fine Arts Gallery in Balboa Park, the home of the San Diego Fine Arts Society, is an excellent small gallery, specializing in paintings of the Spanish school. One of its choice possessions is a *St. Francis* by El Greco. Permanent and loan exhibits are offered the year round. Because of San Diego's natural beauty, artists have made it a mecca for more than half a century. Seascapes are favorite subjects, and the cliffs and caves of La Jolla are particularly attractive to visiting artists. The resident artists, and those who live here part of the year, have the time to explore the back country, and find many landscape subjects. Among the older generation, Charles Reiffel is perhaps the best known. (See illustration, p. 55.) Examples of his land- and seascapes are to be found in many American galleries. Herman Fries and Maurice Braun also have attained national prominence. Among the younger artists of growing national fame is Donal Hord, whose statue, *The Aztec,* cut from diorite, was unveiled on the campus of San Diego State College, May 2, 1937. (See frontispiece.) Numerous art clubs and guilds offer mutual aid, criticism, and encouragement to their members. Most notable of this category is Los Sureños Art Center in Spanish Village, Balboa Park. (See *Tour* 2.)

A growing interest in photography is exemplified by the Photographic Arts Society, which has its own building in Balboa Park. Exhibits of local work and of traveling salons are offered to the public. Throughout the city are camera clubs, and the visual education department of the city schools supervises and aids student camera clubs.

A number of free lance and professional writers have at various times made San Diego their home. Helen Hunt Jackson collected material for *Ramona* while visiting here; and Joaquin Miller, Owen Wister, and Edwin Markham have worked in this area. Among the recent authors who are residents of San Diego and environs are Harold Bell Wright, Stuart Lake, Walt Mason, Alan LeMay, and Max Miller, whose *I Cover the Waterfront* has done as much as the earlier *Ramona* to turn the national eye on San Diego. Besides the three daily newspapers, The San Diego *Union, Evening Tribune,* and The San Diego *Sun,* there are several publications of purely local or southern California interest, such as the *Süd-California Deutsche Zeitung,* a weekly newspaper in German, established in 1887; the *Southern Cross,* official organ of the Roman Catholic Church in the San Diego diocese; the *Southwestern Jewish Review;* and the small but lively publication of the San Diego

GRACE LUTHERAN CHURCH, A FINE EXAMPLE OF COMBINED
SPANISH AND GOTHIC ARCHITECTURE (*Osser Studio photograph*)

Zoological Society, the *Zoonooz*. A unique example of historical local
journalism is the San Diego *Herald,* published between 1851 and 1860,
of which the only extensive file in existence is preserved in the San Diego
Public Library. To the columns of this paper, during 1853, *John Phoenix*
contributed his writings which later became nationally famous in *Phoenixiana,* a book of his collected journalism. (See *Historical: The
Americans.*)

In point of influence and appeal, radios are as indicative of a
community as the newspapers. Two local stations, KGB and KFSD,
offer the programs of the national networks. Across the border, in
Tijuana, are seven stations. Programs of these stations are uniformly
alike. Popular dance and song programs, in English and Spanish,
advertise local merchants; the music, for the most part, is from records.
Quack programs are frequent, offering leases on possible oil land, hitherto
unknown medical panaceas, and many varieties of fortune tellers including
astrologers. Because these stations are not within the jurisdiction of the
Federal Communications Commission they can broadcast programs, barred
from the American stations, over powerful transmitters which cover the
Pacific coast.

San Diego's school system, in a state whose educational facilities are
conceded to be above average, has been rated second highest in California.
San Diego State College, a regional college under the State Director of
Education, was established in 1887 and in 1931 moved to its new 125-
acre tract where the campus and buildings, still in the process of
construction, are designed in a modified Spanish-Moorish style of
architecture.

Among educational organizations of a private nature, the San Diego
Open Forum is exceptional. Without having had a break in schedule
throughout the depression, this organization offers eight months of lecture
courses annually from October to May. The board of directors presents

outstanding speakers on subjects of national importance, and in the past has obtained such lecturers as Upton Close, Maude Royden, Sherwood Eddy, Maurice Hindus, Robert Millikan, Stewart Chase, and Will Durant. A small charge to the members of the society covers the running expenses, which is augmented by a collection at the meetings.

The San Diego Public Library has one of the highest ratings among the 44 libraries in the United States in cities of one hundred thousand to two hundred thousand population range. There are approximately one hundred and sixty thousand volumes in the collection, and registered borrowers number 75,148. For the year 1935-36, the volume circulation was 1,342,130, which made a per capita circulation of eight volumes. Recently there has been a decreased demand for recreational and time-filling books and an increasing demand for periodicals and books on vocational subjects.

Churches are a noticeable element in San Diego's social pattern. There are slightly less than one hundred and fifty, and thus about one to each one thousand persons. The Roman Catholic churches serve one-fifth of the population. The Theosophical Society and Universal Brotherhood, on Point Loma, attracts members from all over the world. Christian Science is well represented, as well as smaller groups such as Rosicrucians, Spiritualists, and Unity followers. Racial minority groups maintain their own churches. Architecturally, the majority of churches are ordinary, but an important exception is the Spanish Gothic Grace Lutheran Church, Lincoln Avenue and Park Boulevard. (See illustration, p. 61.) This admirably designed building, the work of Architects Albert Schroeder and Frederick Kennedy, won several awards in 1930, the year of its completion. Another structure, Our Lady of the Rosary, church of the Italian colony, has become nationally famous for its paintings, murals, and brilliant stained glass windows. These were made by Fausto Tasta, a Venetian painter and sculptor, who worked on the church for 3 years.

On the whole, San Diego is an architectural composite. The Spanish Mission or Monterey style developed by Serra, and the Spanish Colonial, which the Spanish and Mexicans brought into California, was almost eradicated by the early American occupation. During the 1870's, 1880's, and 1890's, most of the buildings were of the sturdy New England and middle western frame type. The inevitable "gingerbread" style of the turn of the century gained a strong footing in San Diego, as may be seen in a majority of the older residences and business blocks. With the Exposition of 1915, through the efforts of Bertram Goodhue, there was a revival of interest in the Spanish heritage. Since that time there has been a statewide interest in Spanish Colonial architecture. A few of the original adobe houses in Old Town have been preserved. The Bandini House, a good example of the Monterey style, has been recently restored and is again, after a half century, used as a rooming house. (See *Tour* 1.) Around Fifth Avenue and Market Street are still to be seen the two- and three-storied buildings which were, in the 1870's, the last word in modernism. Today, 12-storied buildings, mainly constructed during the 1920's, give a modern skyline to the business area. There has also been a distinct tendency the past year to remodel smaller buildings and put modern fronts on them. The tax-rate on larger buildings at the present time has seemed prohibitive to the prospective builder. In the newer residential districts, Mission Hills, Point Loma, La Jolla, and Loma Portal, the tendency has been toward the Spanish type homes.

In contrast to the cultural interests of San Diego is the widespread interest in sports and recreation. Stimulated by the comparatively large number of tourists, visitors, and retired residents who seek entertainment and diversion the year round, and augmented by the many thousands of enlisted men of the United States armed forces who are stationed here, outdoor recreations are practicable almost every day of the year. Motoring is particularly popular locally because of the smooth highways and excellent natural setting. The ratio of cars to population is quite high, there being 99,000 motor vehicles registered in San Diego County. Mountains, seashore, and city recreational areas are all within easy reach of the pleasure seeker. Aquatic sports predominate in the immediate environs. Fishing barges are anchored just off shore during the season, and boats ply regularly between San Diego and the fishing banks at sea. Anglers may try their luck along the surf and from the piers, and the devotee of fresh water fishing may go to the reservoirs and lakes in the mountainous back country. About the bay are yacht harbors, and small boats are offered for rent.

Roller skating, dancing, and motorcycling are prime diversions for service men. Baseball, both professional and semiprofessional, including night softball, is the most popular sport in San Diego from the point of view of the spectator. So popular is baseball that during the 1936 season games played on the home diamond by the San Diego Padres of the Pacific Coast League drew greater attendance than did the same Coast League games at Los Angeles and San Francisco, notwithstanding the fact the population of those cities is many times greater than that of San Diego.

Hiking trails and precipitous mountain paths are numerous in the county. Bridle trails and horseback trips vary from the wooded hills of Balboa Park to the mountain trails 50 miles eastward, through the gorge of Mission Valley. Game for hunting, though not so plentiful as in bygone years, is still sufficient in the back country to attract the hunter. Signposted areas have been set aside in the Cleveland National Forest, and in certain other portions of the county, in which no hunting is allowed.

While San Diego cannot be compared with such metropolitan areas as Chicago, New York, or San Francisco for the production and fostering of cultural activities, the varied natural scene and the equable climate have drawn people with means for leisurely enjoyment of life to San Diego. At present the interest in outdoor activities is dominant, and, as would be expected, equalized throughout the community. Cultural activities are maintained by smaller and more exclusive elements, but there is a noticeably growing tendency to make the arts and music an integral part of unified community life.

CHRONOLOGY

1542 Sept. 28	Juan Rodríguez Cabrillo discovers San Diego Bay and names it San Miguel.
1602 Nov. 10	Don Sebastian Vizcaíno enters the harbor and names it for San Diego de Alcalá.
1769 Apr. 11	The *San Antonio,* under the command of Don Juan Pérez, lands the first colonists for the province of Alta California.
May 14	Rivera and Fages, with a command of troops, arrive overland from Mexico.
July 16	Fr. Junípero Serra dedicates a little hut on Presidio Hill as Mission San Diego de Alcalá.
1770 Mar. 19	Arrival of the *San Antonio* with food saves the colony from starvation.
1774 In August	The foundations laid for a new mission building 6 miles up Mission Valley from Presidio Hill.
1775 Nov. 4	Diegueño Indians on the warpath, 800 strong, sack and fire the new mission, killing Fr. Jayme.
1793 Nov. 27	The British ship *Discovery* under command of George Vancouver is the first foreign vessel to enter San Diego Bay.
1795 In July	Manuel de Vargas, pioneer school teacher of the state, opens the first public school.
1798,	Four sailors, left in Baja California by the American ship *Gallant,* trek overland and are the first Americans to enter San Diego.
1800 Aug. 25	The *Betsy,* under the command of Capt. Charles Winship, is the first American ship to enter port.
1803 Mar. 17	The *Lelia Byrd,* an American ship under command of Capt. Wm. Shaler, attempts to leave port with 1,000 smuggled otter skins. The Spanish garrison at Ballast Point opens fire; the *Lelia Byrd* returns it and sails out. No casualties.
1817 In Mar.	The *Traveler* departs with California's first shipment of grain.
1822 Apr. 20	Spanish rule overthrown; the Mexican flag is raised.
1834 Sept. 1	Don Juan Bandini and José Hijar arrive on the brig *Natalie* with 140 colonists.
1835 Jan. 1	The first town council is organized.
1846 July 29	At the command of Colonel Frémont, Lieutenant Rowan of the sloop of war *Cyane* raises the United States flag at Old Town.
Sept. 15	Commodore Stockton orders an American election.
Dec. 6	Brig. Gen. S. W. Kearny and American troops meet Gen. Andrés Pico and his Mexican-Californian army at San Pasqual. Stockton's timely aid saves the day.
1848 Feb. 2	Under the terms of the treaty of Guadalupe Hidalgo,

	San Diego becomes a port of entry for the United States.
1849 Feb. 13	The international boundary survey of the line between Mexico and the United States is ordered.
1850 Feb. 18	The legislative act making San Diego one of the original twenty-seven counties is signed by Governor Burnett.
Apr. 1	With much excitement the first county election is held. Citizens turn out and cast their 157 votes.
1851 May 29	San Diego feels important enough to have a newspaper. The *Herald* is founded.
June 20	In the old Exchange Hotel, the Masons hold their first meeting in San Diego.
1852 Feb. 26	A military reservation is created on Point Loma.
Mar. 25	Due to repeal of the charter of 1850 an election is held. A board of trustees without taxing power is elected.
1853 July 10	The first services of the Episcopalian church are held in Old Town, presided over by the Rev. John Reynolds.
1854 July 1	A public school is opened.
1855 Nov. 15	The Old Spanish Lighthouse on Point Loma begins its brief career.
1857 Aug. 13	The schooner *Loma* is launched, the first boat to be built in San Diego shipyards.
Aug. 31	Stage driver James E. Mason brings the first overland mail to town. He likes the town and stays to help it grow.
1867 Apr. 15	"Father" Alonzo E. Horton, founder of New San Diego, arrives on board the steamer *Pacific*.
Apr. 30	The first Board of Trustees, selected by Horton, meets.
May 10	Alonzo Horton pays $265 for the land on which he founds New San Diego, now the heart of the city.
May 26	The Board of Trustees sets aside 320 acres for a city park. Later additions bring the park, Balboa Park, to approximately 1,400 acres.
Oct. 10	San Diego is growing; The San Diego *Weekly Union* begins publication.
1869 Apr. 8	The first post office is established, and Jacob Allen is appointed postmaster.
May 17	We now have a fire department.
1870 Jan. 22	Horton's new town is growing rapidly. The San Diego Chamber of Commerce is organized, Aaron Pauly elected president.
Jan. 24	The first public library is founded with the donation of a single pamphlet (lecture before the Bunker Hill Association), and with the promise of 600 volumes from Alonzo Horton. Years later Mr. Horton delivered his gift.

Feb. 13	The first Methodist Church opens at 4th and Broadway.
In June	Alonzo Horton becomes president of the Bank of San Diego, the city's first bank.
Oct. 17	Alonzo Horton believes in his city. He builds and opens his hotel, *Horton House,* with pomp and celebration. Everyone is there.
1871 Mar. 20	The San Diego *Weekly Union* becomes a daily, with Douglas Gunn in the editor's chair.
Apr. 21	A floating bathhouse, *The Cosoy,* founders in the bay.
Aug. 12	Impressive ceremonies mark the laying of the cornerstone of the new courthouse.
1872 Apr. 20	Old Town is swept by a fire which destroys the business district. New San Diego will have no more competition from that source.
Apr. 25	Nine bars of gold valued at $10,000, product of eleven days' run, brought to San Diego from the Julian Mines.
1873 Jan. 20	The San Diego Water Company is incorporated and bores for artesian water. It looks as though the water problem is going to be solved.
1874 Apr. 1	After years of dispute about the city area, the Federal Government grants a patent right for 11 square leagues of land (48,556.69 acres).
1876 Apr. 7	New charter is granted giving trustees taxing power and increasing their number to five.
1877 Dec. 5	Lieutenant Reade, of the United States Weather Bureau, gives the first public demonstration of the telephone.
1881 July 19	The San Diego *Sun* commences publication.
1882 Jan. 12	A snowstorm plays havoc with flocks of sheep within the city limits. Thousands die of exposure.
In Mar.	The Y.M.C.A. opens a branch.
1885 Nov. 21	San Diego is definitely on the map—the Santa Fe R.R. brings in its first train from the East.
1886 Mar. 16	With the installation of electric lights, San Diego enters the Electric Age.
May 13	Reincorporation by vote of the people, with no change in governmental form.
In May	There has been intense opposition to the new city charter, but it is adopted.
July 4	To celebrate the nation's birthday, the first horse-drawn streetcar system begins operation over the two-mile track on Broadway.
1887 Jan. 1	The National City & Otay R.R., a steam train line, begins operation.
In Nov.	Electric streetcar service begins operation between San Diego and Old Town.

1888 In Mar.	Sweetwater Dam, an engineering feat of great importance, is completed.
1889 Feb. 22	The flume line is opened which is to bring San Diego River water into the city.
Mar. 2	New city charter ratified.
1891 May 6	Chilean insurgent transport, the *Itata,* seized at San Diego.
1892 Sept. 28-30	San Diego, conscious of its venerable age, celebrates the 350th anniversary of Cabrillo's discovery.
1893 Mar. 11	Riverside County created; carving a large slice from the northern part of San Diego County.
1895 Dec. 21	*Evening Tribune* begins publication.
1897 Mar. 13	The governor signs a legislative measure which establishes a State Normal School at San Diego.
1899 Jan. 21	With the arrival of the *Belgian King*, of the California & Oriental Steamship Co., San Diego begins a bid for world shipping.
1901 July 21	The municipality purchases all water systems within the city for $600,000. Bonds are voted for the purpose.
1903-1904	The County Hospital is built, unit at a time.
1905 July 21	In the midst of a festive leave-taking, the boilers on U.S. Gunboat *Bennington* explode. Sixty are killed; 47 injured. Bennington Cemetery is established on Point Loma and a public mass burial is held on July 23.
1906 Dec. 14	The Spreckels interests form a corporation to build the San Diego & Arizona R.R. Capital: $6,000,000.
1907 Aug. 15	Imperial County created; San Diego County losing 4,089 sq. miles by this act.
1908 July 26	Automobiles are becoming a problem. The City Council passes the first traffic ordinance.
1911 Jan. 26	Creating aviation history, Glenn H. Curtiss raises a hydroplane from San Diego Bay.
Nov. 4	Harbor development is assured with the voting of a $1,000,000 bond issue.
1912 May 14	The "free speech" fight staged by the I.W.W. is broken when Emma Goldman leaves town and Ben Reitman is tarred and feathered.
Sept. 28	The Masons dedicate Al Bahr Temple with about 700 members participating in the ceremony.
1913 Feb. 1	The city's water system grows with the purchase of the Southern California Mountain Water Co., for $2,509,375.
1914 May 5	Morena Dam purchased for $1,500,000.
Dec. 16	An eight-foot tide creates a record for San Diego.
1915 Jan. 1	The Panama-California Exposition is dedicated.
May 31	The San Diego Stadium is formally opened and is hailed as the world's largest municipal structure.
July 17	Wm. Jennings Bryan visits the Exposition.

July 26	Theodore Roosevelt and wife visit the Exposition.
July 28	The first battleships to enter San Diego Bay, the *Missouri, Ohio,* and *Wisconsin,* arrive.
Oct. 29	Thomas A. Edison and Henry Ford visit the Exposition.
Nov. 12	The Liberty Bell is exhibited at the Exposition for three days.
Dec. 13	Telephone service is established between New York and San Diego.
1916 Jan. 27	Lower Otay Dam washes out; the unusual rains cause an estimated damage of $4,000,000 over the county.
1917 Jan. 27	The Navy opens the most powerful radio station in the Western Hemisphere at Chollas Heights.
Sept. 5	The first drafted troops for service in the World War entrain for camp.
1918 Jan. 24	Contracts totaling more than $6,000,000 are awarded for construction work at North Island and Fort Rosecrans.
June 9	Federal building activities get under way, totaling $19,000,000.
Dec. 3	Three members of the Board of Education recalled.
Dec. 9	The first airmail service is established.
1919 Mar. 15	The Marine Base becomes a reality with the ground-breaking ceremonies. Six congressmen are present.
July 17	North Island becomes the official base for west coast air activities.
Sept. 1	Lower Otay (Savage) Dam is dedicated, which replaces the dam that washed out.
Nov. 15	The San Diego & Arizona R.R. is completed, and John D. Spreckels drives a golden spike in the last tie.
1920 Feb. 2	San Diego is restored as a port of entry.
Apr. 7	Edward, Prince of Wales, addresses 25,000 enthusiastic citizens in the city stadium.
June 22	The Federal census informs the world that San Diego has a population of 74,683.
Nov. 1	Contracts awarded for the building of the Naval Hospital.
1922 Feb. 26	Evangeline Booth, head of the Salvation Army, addresses a record audience.
Apr. 17	The Union-Tribune Southern Electrical Broadcasting Station begins operation.
May 10	Mr. and Mrs. A. S. Bridges present the city with the Museum of Fine Arts.
June 7	Rancho Santa Fe is opened for settlement.
June 12	A reference library of scientific literature is assured the city with the gift of $30,000 from W. W. Whitney, local merchant.
July 25	Barrett Dam is dedicated.
Sept. 5	Flying from Jacksonville, Florida, Lieut. James H.

	Doolittle sets a coast-to-coast record of 21 hours and 19 minutes.
Oct. 6	Lieuts. Oakley Kelley and John Macready set a sustained flight record by remaining in the air for 35 hours and 18 minutes.
1923 In Apr.	John D. Spreckels gives the San Diego Zoo a brace of elephants.
June 1	The Naval Training Station is officially commissioned.
1924 July 1	A new electric railway line, costing $3,500,000, begins operations to La Jolla.
Sept. 22	The first aviation circumnavigation of the globe is completed when Lieuts. Lowell Smith, Eric Nelson, and Leigh Wade land their planes at San Diego.
Oct. 10	The *Shenandoah* arrives, having made the first dirigible airship transcontinental flight.
1925 Mar. 12	The combined east and west coast battle fleet is anchored in the bay and in the Coronado Roads.
1926 Oct. 19	A $2,000,000 bond issue is voted to build Sutherland Dam. After large expenditures the site is abandoned.
1927 May 10	Charles Lindbergh, a young aviation enthusiast, hops off for St. Louis in his new San Diego-built plane, *Spirit of St. Louis*.
May 21	San Diego celebrates the completion of Lindbergh's flight to Paris.
1928 Aug. 14	A mass flight of 135 airplanes over North Island is reviewed by Secretary of the Navy Curtis Wilbur.
Aug. 16	Lindbergh Field is dedicated.
1929 Jan. 2	Aviation history is made again with the first plane refueling by night.
Nov. 8	The new Fox Theatre is dedicated. It cost $1,800,000.
1930 Jan. 12	A new sustained flight record for gliders is established by W. H. Bowlus.
June 12	Regular airmail service is established with the north and east.
Dec. 31	Dr. Albert Einstein visits San Diego.
1931 Feb. 16	The new San Diego State College is dedicated. It cost $750,000.
Apr. 7	New city charter is adopted at a general election, replacing the one of 1889.
1934 Sept. 22	The California Institute of Technology acquires 160 acres on Mt. Palomar for the future home of the world's largest telescope.
1935 Feb. 22	El Capitan Dam dedicated. Capacity: 38 billion gallons. Cost: $5,790,000.
May 28	The California Pacific International Exposition opens with a first day attendance of 60,000.
Aug. 23	With 87 first-line naval vessels steaming into the

	harbor, and 416 fighting planes circling the sky, San Diego witnesses a water and air parade.
Sept. 14	San Diego leads the west coast cities in bank cash gains according to clearing house reports for the month of August.
Oct. 2	President Franklin Delano Roosevelt addresses the largest audience ever assembled in the city stadium.
Oct. 20	The Consolidated Aircraft Corp. dedicates its new plant.
Dec. 5	Ground-breaking ceremonies for the San Diego Civic Center are held on the bay front.
Dec. 10	Federal funds received for improving Mission Bay State Park.
1936 Jan. 22	Federal approval for construction of the County Fair Grounds at Del Mar received.
Feb. 12	The California Pacific International Exposition re-opens for a second year.
Nov. 21	Funeral rites held for Mme. Schumann-Heink, famous singer.
1937 Feb. 3	The Right Rev. Buddy is installed as Bishop of the newly created Diocese of San Diego, Roman Catholic church.
June 24-25	Richard Archbold makes the first transcontinental non-stop flight in a seaplane, taking 17 hrs. and 3 min. to travel from San Diego to New York City.
Oct. 18	Gov. Frank F. Merriam dedicates divided highway unit on El Cajon Blvd. (US 80.)
Dec. 1	A semiofficial estimate places the city's population at 183,800.

LIST OF TOURS

TOURS IN THE CITY

Tour 1 Old Town   -   3   *m.*   72

     2 Point Loma   -   9   *m.*   78

     3 Balboa Park   -   4   *m.*   83

     4 The Waterfront   -   25   *m.*   90

     5 Beach Towns   - 24.1   *m.*   95

TOURS IN ENVIRONS

Tour 6 Coronado-Old Mexico   99

     7 Old Missions   102

        Side Tour 7A Palomar Observatory   108

     8 The Back Country   112

        Side Tour 8A The Desert   118

     9 Campo Road   123

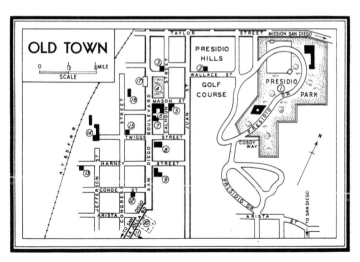

TOURS IN THE CITY

TOUR 1 — 3 *m.*

OLD TOWN

NW. from Trias St. on Fort Stockton Dr.; L. from Fort Stockton Dr. on Arista Dr.; R. from Arista Dr. on Presidio Dr.

Presidio Hill Park, identified with San Diego's founding, is the birthplace of California civilization. Within the park are remnants of the Spanish occupation—portions of the walls and residences of the *presidio* (Sp., *garrison*), an ancient brass cannon, and a museum containing relics of the early days.

Below the hill is Old Town (Sp., *El Pueblo de San Diego Viejo*), built on the river flats, where soldiers of the *presidio* established home sites. Capt. Francisco María Ruiz is credited with building the first adobe house on that site about 1820. As more soldiers and settlers came from Mexico, this outpost grew into a town. By 1829 there were about 30 houses; and at the time of the American occupation the town had more than six hundred population.

A fire in 1872 destroyed many of the buildings in Old Town, and the community never recovered its former importance. Horton's Addition, a new section then being developed on the site of the present business area of San Diego, profited by this fire. (See *Historical: The Americans.*)

The oldest cemetery in the San Diego area, formerly on Presidio Hill, has long since been obliterated.

1. PRESIDIO HILL PARK, Presidio Dr. at intersection of Twiggs St. and Cosoy Way, is a tract of about 37 acres, presented to the city by George W. Marston in 1929, and accepted officially in July, 1937. John Nolen, city planning expert, began the landscaping which has been carried on since 1932 by P. C. Broell. Within this area are several relics of Spanish, Mexican, and early American occupation.

The SITE OF FORT STOCKTON, approached by a stairway a short distance from the entrance of the park (L), is on a shoulder of Presidio Hill overlooking Old Town. In 1838 a small fort was built on this spot by the Mexican townsfolk as a defense against an anticipated Indian attack. Its strategic position led Comdr. Samuel Dupont to occupy it when he landed American forces in 1846. At that time it was strengthened and named in his honor. In November of that year Comdr. Robert F. Stockton took command. A deep trench was dug around the fort, and on the earth embankment were placed barrels filled with stone and rubble. Cannon were mounted between the barrels. After these alterations the fort was called Fort Stockton. The trench is still visible, roughly outlining a quadrangle. Inside this area stands *El Jupiter,* a Spanish cannon which was cast in Manila in 1783.

PALOU MONUMENT, R. of Fort Stockton in the center of an open green at the foot of an evergreen tree is a bronze plaque commemorating Padre Palou, co-worker and biographer of Padre Serra. His published

SERRA MUSEUM, OVERLOOKING OLD
TOWN *(Wahrenbrock photograph)*

account of the establishment of Alta California is one of the most important authorities on the early Spanish colonization.

SERRA MUSEUM, 2727 Presidio Dr. (*open Tues.-Sat., 10-5 p.m., Sun., 1-5 p.m.; free*), was built by George W. Marston in 1929 and presented to the city. It is in charge of the San Diego Historical Society and exhibits collections of local historic interest, including firearms, branding irons, saddles, bridles, riatas and other relics of California's pastoral era. The building is of Spanish Mission architecture, with white stucco walls, deep-set windows, and red tiled roof. A square tower rises above the north end of the structure and from the south end extends an arcade.

The SITE OF EL PRESIDIO REAL (Sp., *The Royal Garrison*), is in front of the Serra Museum. Within a hollow square which has been surrounded by a modern adobe wall are some mounds and occasional bits of adobe wall, marking the ground plan of the original buildings. Typical of most Spanish and Mexican presidios, there was the chapel, the comandante's house, storehouses, and living quarters for officers, soldiers, and their families. Originally established in 1769, the first outpost of Spain's endeavor to save California from encroachments of foreign powers, it was used for garrison purposes until 1835. A tiny presidial chapel, in which Padre Serra officiated, was the first mission establishment in Upper California. In 1774 the mission was moved 6 miles up Mission Valley to its present location. (See *Tour 7.*)

JUNIPERO SERRA CROSS, in the center of the presidio, was built in 1913 from bits of brick and floor tile found on the site. These old bricks were made by the Indian neopyhtes under the supervision of the padres. A bronze plaque at the base of the cross bears an inscription by the society which erected the monument. Three ancient palm trees were transplanted to the mound in 1929.

To the right is the best preserved section of the *presidio* area. In the clearing in front of the mounds is a bronze statue, *The Indian,* by Arthur Putnam, a Californian. A concrete observation platform is behind the statue, from which point is seen the full sweep of Mission Valley and the meager San Diego River. At one time the river's course turned at the foot of Presidio Hill and the river emptied into San Diego Bay, but in 1853-55 the Federal government built the DERBY DIKE (L), which turned the river into Mission Bay. This work was supervised by Lieut. George H. Derby, whose literary antics, published in the old San Diego *Herald* under the pen name of John Phoenix, achieved national renown.

SERRA PALM TREE, on the river flats below (L), is thought to have been planted in 1769 by Padre Serra. It marks the approximate burial place of more than 60 soldiers and sailors who died of scurvy on the sea expedition of 1769. (See *Historical: The Spanish.*) This tree also marks the beginning of *El Camino Real* (Sp., *The Royal Highway*), which was the road traced by Governor Portolá when he set out for Monterey on July 14, 1769. This highway was used by the padres when they established the other missions.

L. on Presidio Dr. to Wallace St.; R. on Wallace St.

2. CASA DE CARRILLO, 4136 Wallace St. (Sp., *Carrillo's House*)

(*open; free*), a four-room house, box-like in shape, with tile roof, recently restored, is thought to be the original house built in the first quarter of the nineteenth century by Captain Ruiz. In the 1830's it was given to the San Diego branch of the Carrillo family and was occupied by them. It is also known as the Pear Garden House, because a pear orchard, supposed to have been the first private orchard in California, surrounded the house. It stands on the Presidio Hill Golf Course and is used as a clubhouse.

3. CONGRESS HALL, cor. Calhoun and Wallace Sts. (*private*), is a barnlike wooden structure also known as the French Bakery. It stood originally on another side of the plaza and was used as a bakery. About 1870 it was remodeled and became Congress Hall, one of Old Town's most important hotels, saloons, and gambling houses. It was moved to its present site after 1876, where it became a post office and station of the Pony Express.

4. OLD TOWN PLAZA, a small park, bounded by Wallace St., Calhoun St., Mason St., and San Diego Ave., was the center of town activities. Around it the earliest homes and stores were built. A white flagpole stands in the center of the square, its bronze marker indicating that the first United States flag was raised officially at this point in 1846. An old Spanish cannon, EL CAPITAN (Sp., *The Captain*), is near the flagpole, a companion piece to EL JUPITER in Fort Stockton. In the northeast corner of the plaza is a boulder with another bronze marker which indicates the end of the Kearny Trail, the road from Fort Leavenworth, Kansas, over which Kearny led the American troops in 1846. (See *Historical: The Americans.*) In the southeast corner is a MEMORIAL BENCH which honors Tommy Getz, the San Diegan who preserved the Estudillo House and made it a museum of Old Town relics. *L. on Mason St. to Calhoun St.; R. on Calhoun St.*

5. CASA DE BANDINI, 2660 Calhoun St. (*private*), was a one-storied adobe house when built in 1829. Don Juan Bandini, the owner, favored the Americans in the California War, and offered his house to Commodore Stockton as headquarters in 1846-47. It was here that Kit Carson found him when he brought General Kearny's plea for aid from the San Pasqual battlefield. (See *Tour 7A.*) Late in 1869 a second story was added and a balcony put around two sides, characteristic of the Monterey style; and for several years it was operated as the Cosmopolitan Hotel. Owned at the present time by a grandson of Juan Bandini, it has been restored and is being used as a rooming house. *Retrace Calhoun St. to Mason St.; L. on Mason St.*

6. CASA DE ESTUDILLO, Mason St. bet. Calhoun St. and San Diego Ave. (*open daily*, 8:30-5:30 *p.m.; adm.* 10c), is popularly known as Ramona's Marriage Place. Built about 1828 by Don Jose Antonio Estudillo, this adobe house was used by his family until 1887. The house is of adobe construction with walls from two to four feet thick. The tiled roof is supported by heavy rough-hewn timbers, brought down from the distant mountains on the backs of Mission Indians. The beams are bound together with rawhide thongs, no nails being used. The legend that Ramona was married here, fostered for commercial purposes, is unfounded. The place described in Helen Hunt Jackson's book

Ramona as the marriage place is the Adobe Chapel. The Estudillo House stood unoccupied and in ruins until about 1910, when it was restored by the Spreckels interests. Tommy Getz then operated it as a museum of early Californiana. It is the outstanding landmark of Old Town, and its 12 rooms, large garden patio, paintings and furniture, and the family chapel help to recreate the atmosphere of the old Mexican village.

L. from Mason St. on San Diego Ave.; which becomes La Jolla Ave.

7.   CASA DE PEDRORENA, 2616 San Diego Ave. (*private*), was built about 1838 by Don Miguel de Pedrorena and became the home of his daughter and her husband, Jose Antonio Altamirano. Pedrorena favored the Americans in the war of 1846, and it was in this back yard that the cannon *El Jupiter* was buried to prevent its falling into the hands of the Mexican forces. Pedrorena was also one of the founders of New San Diego. (*See Historical: The Americans.*)   The ornate porch which covers the front of this adobe house was put on during the 1890's but the rear of the building shows quite well the adobe structure.

To the right of the Pedrorena House is a small FRAME HOUSE (*private*), also built by Pedrorena. This was the first home of The San Diego *Union,* and from it the paper was issued between 1868 and 1870.

8.   CHURCH OF THE IMMACULATE CONCEPTION, NE. cor. San Diego Ave. and Twiggs St., (*open*), is the Roman Catholic church for this area. The building was started in 1868 but not completed until 1919. It follows closely the designs made for it by Father Antonio Ubàch which were selected from the best examples of California Mission architecture, with massive stucco walls, red tiled roof, and campanile. The bells were cast of metal from six of the earliest California bells and contain much silver. In the vestibule are several old statues of the saints and three oil paintings. Two of the paintings, a *Last Judgment* and a *Virgin Mary,* are both executed in the early Renaissance manner, and the third, *San Diego de Alcalá,* the patron saint of San Diego, is an excellent example of church portraiture. The paintings are anonymous.

9.   WHALEY HOUSE, NE. cor. San Diego Ave. and Harney St. (*private*), the first modern brick building in San Diego, is of two-story construction, covering about 20x35 feet of ground. Built by Thomas Whaley in 1856, with bricks he manufactured, it was used as a home and store. Extremely hard plaster was made from ground sea shells and the wood used in the structure was brought around Cape Horn. This building has been the residence of the Whaley family since its construction. For a short time during the 1860's a portion of the house was used as the San Diego county court house. On this site in 1851 a man named "Yankee Jim" Robinson was hanged for stealing a rowboat.

10.   EL CAMPO SANTO (Sp., *the cemetery*), bet. Conde and Ampudia Sts. (*open*), was the Roman Catholic burial ground between 1850 and 1880. The ground was at first the private property of the Pedrorena family, and for several years after it became a burial ground permission of the family was necessary for the use of it. A garden adobe wall has been built around the plot, and the few identifiable graves have been re-marked. According to the burial book of the church, more than six hundred persons are buried in this small area.

11.   The SITE OF THE COBBLESTONE JAIL, bet. Conde and Ampu-

dia Sts. (*private*), is marked by a heap of cobblestones and rubble. Built by Agostin Haraszthy, it was San Diego's first large graft job. (See *Historical:The Americans*). Failing to be of any use as a jail, it was utilized as San Diego's first county hospital for several years in the 1860's. It will be restored by the city in the near future.

Retrace La Jolla St. to Conde St.; L. on Conde St.

12. ADOBE CHAPEL, bet. San Diego Ave. and Congress St. (*open*), was the marriage place of Ramona. Built in 1850 by John Brown, an early American settler and cattle raiser, it served as his town home for many years. There is a tradition that it was a saloon, "The Jolly House," during the middle 1850's, but there is little fact to substantiate this. In 1858 it was purchased by José Antonio Agüirre, one of the wealthiest Spanish citizens of Old Town, who remodeled it for church purposes. It was dedicated in November, 1858, as the Church of the Immaculate Conception. Agüirre died in 1860 and is buried in the south wing of the building. In the late 1860's Father Antonio Ubach became the officiating priest, holding this position until his death in 1907. Helen Hunt Jackson visited Ubach when gathering material for her magazine articles on the missions, and he told her of a half-breed Indian and a white girl who came to him for marriage. This tale became part of the *Ramona* legend. Ubach himself became the prototype of *Father Gasparra* in her book. The present restoration of the adobe building was accomplished through W. P. A.

R. from Conde St. on Congress St.; L. from Congress St. on Harney St.

13. DERBY HOUSE, 3877 Harney St. (*private*), is also known as the Pendleton House. Built about 1852 by Don Juan Bandini, it was given to his daughter and her American husband, Capt. Charles Johnson, for a residence. The building is composed of two units, a two-storied front section of frame and a rear portion of adobe. Lieut. George H. Derby lived in this house from 1853 to 1855 while supervising the construction of Derby Dike. From his upper bedroom window he could watch the progress of workmen, thus avoiding too frequent trips across the river flats. It was here that he wrote the majority of the *Phoenixiana* papers upon which his fame rests. This property was purchased in the 1860's by George Pendleton, county clerk and recorder, and until his death in 1871 the house was used as a recorder's office. The house has been carefully restored by the present owner.

Retrace Harney St. to Congress St.; L. on Congress St. to Twiggs St.; L. on Twiggs St.

14. CASA DE LOPEZ, 3800 Twiggs St. (*open by permission*), was built before 1850 and was used by a branch of the Lopez family. Its site gives a commanding view of Old Town to the front. In the early days it was backed by the San Diego River, which ran where the railroad track is now. Standing in an isolated position, the Lopez House looks as though it had been untouched for the past century and remains one of the least impressive of the larger early adobes, being but a series of square, unconnecting rooms which open upon front and rear porches. It is used as the clubhouse of the riding academy which has its stables in the rear.

Retrace Twiggs St. to Congress St.; L. on Congress St.

77

15. CASA DE COTA, NW. cor. Congress and Twiggs Sts. (*private*), is a two-room fragment of an adobe house which is rapidly falling into ruin. Above an interior doorway is the date 1852, approximately the year of construction.

16. CASA DE STEWART, Congress St. beyond Mason St. (*private*), was supposedly built in the 1830's by Corp. José Manuel Machado, of the presidial force. In the early 1840's his daughter Rosa married John C. Stewart, a shipmate of Richard Henry Dana, Jr. The Stewart family has retained possession of the adobe house. The clapboard siding covering the adobe walls is an alteration of the late nineteenth century. *Retrace Congress St. to Mason St.; L. on Mason St. to San Diego Ave.; L. on San Diego Ave.*

17. CASA DE MACHADO, 2745 San Diego Ave. (*open by permission*), is one of the best preserved of the old adobe houses. With thick walls and tiled roof it is built in reversed L-shape, the rooms opening at the rear into a semi-enclosed garden patio. There is a tradition that this house was built in 1831 by Corp. José Manuel Machado for a daughter, María Antonia Machado de Silvas. During the Mexican War, when it appeared that the Americans were going to capture the town, Señora Silvas rescued the Mexican flag from the plaza and hid it in this house. For this reason the house is also known as the *Casa de la Bandera* (Sp., *House of the flag*).

TOUR 2 — 9 m.
POINT LOMA

W. on Barnett Ave. from the junction with Pacific Hwy.

18. The UNITED STATES MARINE BASE, Barnett Ave. (L) (*open 8-5*), a training station and military base for the United States Marine Corps, was established in 1919 on 300 acres of reclaimed tidelands. An additional 300 acres will be reclaimed soon. Franklin Delano Roosevelt, then Assistant Secretary of the Navy, was one of the principal sponsors. There are 20 permanent buildings at the base, seven of which are barracks, and five sets of officers' quarters.

19. SPEER FLYING FIELD, 3330 Barnett Ave., formerly Ryan Field, is where Charles A. Lindbergh made test flights with the *Spirit of St. Louis* in March, 1927. The field rents planes for either short or long distance flights.

20. The UNITED STATES NAVAL TRAINING STATION, junction of Barnett Ave. and Lytton St. (*open 8-5*), was commissioned on June 1, 1923, and like the marine base, was sponsored by Franklin Delano Roosevelt and Representative Kettner. It is dedicated to the training of recruits and to technical training of naval personnel.

R. from Barnett Ave. on Lytton St.

21. A commercial GOLF COURSE, 2740 Lytton St., is to the right.

22. The LOMA PORTAL residential district, L. of the intersection of Lytton St. and Rosecrans Blvd., was developed after the commissioning of the naval training station to provide homes for the naval officers and their families. It is one of the most modern and best cared for residential sections of San Diego.

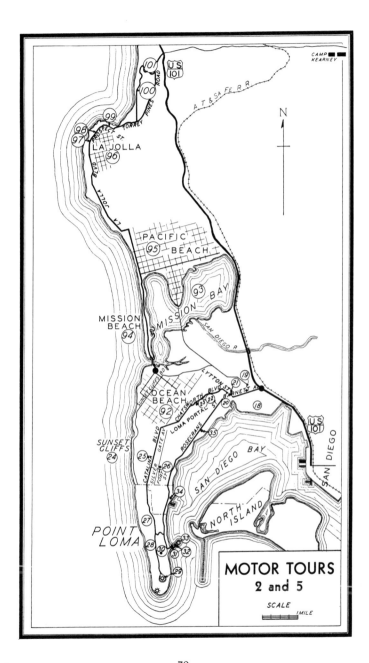

MOTOR TOURS
2 and 5

SCALE
1 MILE

Straight ahead from the junction with Evergreen St.; Lytton St. becomes Chatsworth Blvd.

23. The POINT LOMA HIGH SCHOOL, 2335 Chatsworth Blvd., offers junior and senior high school work for the Point Loma area and the beach towns.

L. from Chatsworth Blvd. on Catalina Blvd.

24. The SUNSET CLIFFS residential district is to the R. (See *Tour* 5.)

25. The INTERNATIONAL HEADQUARTERS OF THE UNIVERSAL BROTHERHOOD AND THEOSOPHICAL SOCIETY, 1 *m.* from the Chatsworth Blvd. junction (*open* 9-5; *adm.* 25c), has a group of buildings on ground purchased by Mme. Katherine Tingley in 1896. The cornerstone of the first building was laid in February 1897. At the death of Madame Tingley in 1929, Dr. G. de Purucker, associated with her for 26 years, succeeded to the headship of the organization. The principal buildings of the Homestead, as the tract is known to the members, are: the Temple of Peace and the Academy, both of Moorish classical architecture; the Greek Theater; the Lomaland School for girls; a school and bungalows for boys; a medical dispensary; a printing office; the former home of A. G. Spalding, noted manufacturer of sporting goods, now used for offices and library; and the home of Doctor de Purucker. Members of the community assist with the work, serving as teachers, printers, sculptors, scientists, musicians, and dramatic producers. The school offers, beside the theosophical groundwork, a wide variety of classical studies.

R. from Catalina Blvd. on Pio Pico St.; R. from Pio Pico St. on Silvergate Ave.

26. The ROSECROFT BEGONIA GARDENS, 530 Silvergate Ave. (*open; adm.* 25c), is a nursery famous for its begonias, said to be the finest collection in the world. More than 400 varieties are grown here, though the nursery also specializes in other types of plants. Seeds and stock for the collection came from all over the world. An interesting specimen of a podocarpus tree, growing here, was raised from seed sent to the owner by Theodore Roosevelt and Stewart Edward White from Africa.

Retrace Silvergate Ave. to Catalina Ave.; R. on Catalina Ave.

27. The UNITED STATES MILITARY RESERVATION, entire southern end of Point Loma (*open* 9-5; *military inspection; no cameras allowed*), was set aside by Congress on Feb. 26, 1852, but was not used until Fort Rosecrans was established in 1870. Fortifications have been constantly added since that date. At the present time (1937) it is considered impregnable. Included in the reservation area is a naval wireless station, Fort Rosecrans, and the old quarantine and coaling station.

28. The BENNINGTON CEMETERY, 1.5 *m.* beyond reservation entrance (*open daily*), was named in honor of the victims of an explosion which occurred on board the United States gunboat *Bennington* in San Diego harbor, July 21, 1905. Here, too, are buried the soldiers and scouts who fell in the battle of San Pasqual, 1846. (See *Historical: The Americans.*)

29. The CABRILLO NATIONAL MONUMENT, end of Catalina Blvd. (*open; free*), popularly known as the Old Spanish Lighthouse, is

HOMESTEAD OF THE THEOSOPHICAL
SOCIETY *(Haase photograph)*

OLD SPANISH LIGHTHOUSE, BEFORE RECENT
RESTORATION *(Public Library photograph)*

the smallest national park in the United States, being about one-half acre. Juan Rodríguez Cabrillo landed on Point Loma in 1542. The lighthouse, built in 1855, is neither Spanish nor Mexican, but American. The popular name was derived from the fact that the early keepers of the light had Mexican wives who spoke only Spanish. Adobe bricks used in its construction were brought up from Ballast Point, below, and were remnants of the old Spanish Fort Guijarros. The light, used until 1891, was abandoned because its elevation rendered it all but useless in times of low fog. The present lighthouse is at sea level on the outer end of Point Loma. The view of San Diego from the Old Spanish Lighthouse is unsurpassed. North Island, Coronado, the Silver Strand, and the mainland from the Mexican border to Mission Valley are spread out below the tower like a gigantic aerial map. At night a myriad of lights and neon signs in the San Diego metropolitan area glitters across the bay and reflects from its placid waters.

Retrace Catalina Blvd. to Alternate Route junction; R. on Alternate Route to Rosecrans Blvd.; R. on Rosecrans Blvd.

30. FORT ROSECRANS, end of Rosecrans Blvd. (*open daily*), has been a permanent army post since 1870, and at present is the home of the 3rd Coast Artillery. At the POST EXCHANGE, just within the gates, information is given concerning parking and visiting at the fort.

L. from Post Exchange on Guijarros Rd.

31. The SITE OF FORT GUIJARROS, on the neck of Ballast Point, bore California's first coastal fortification. Ballast Point, called by the Spanish *La Punta de los Guijarros* (*Cobblestone Point*), was the site of Cabrillo's landing. When Capt. George Vancouver visited San Diego in 1793 he noted the narrow channel into San Diego Bay and remarked that a fortification on Ballast Point would make the harbor a military stronghold. In 1795 plans for fortifying the Point were completed, and during the following decade the fort was built. One of its ten brass cannon may still be seen at Fort Stockton. (See *Tour 1.*) The new fort's one important engagement was with an American trading vessel, the *Lelia Byrd,* which forced her way into the harbor and took on a cargo of otter pelts in defiance of the Spanish law. Fired upon by Fort Guijarros as she was leaving port, the *Lelia Byrd* swung into position, fired a broadside, and scurried out to sea. (See *Historical: The Spanish.*) The fort was abandoned in 1838.

32. The VIZCAINO MARKER, on the neck of Ballast Point, commemorates the landing in 1602 of Sebastian Vizcaíno, who held California's first recorded religious services on this spot, a century and a half prior to the arrival of the padres. Although not mentioned on this plaque, Juan Rodríguez Cabrillo also landed here. It was on the extreme tip of this point that the first coastal beacon in California was lighted— a lantern swung from the top of a pole, used for signaling vessels bound north, in 1769. The first white men to be buried in California lie in the area where Fort Rosecrans now stands.

33. The BALLAST POINT LIGHTHOUSE AREA, end of Ballast Point (*open 1-4, except Sunday; free*), is the site of the old whaling station, which recalls one of San Diego's major industries in the first half of the nineteenth century. At that time San Diego Bay was a

favorite calving ground for whales, and historians inform us that as late as 1840 the bay was so alive with whales that it was dangerous to cross to North Island by boat, as many as 40 having been counted at one time. *Retrace Guijarros Rd. to Rosecrans Blvd.; R. on Rosecrans Blvd.*

34. The old UNITED STATES NAVAL QUARANTINE and COAL-ING STATION (*open*), is approximately the site of old *LA PLAYA* (Sp., *the beach*), one of the three communities which made up San Diego in the early years of American occupation. La Playa was famous during Spanish times as a recreational beach, but with the advent of Mexican rule it became the center of the hide and tallow industry, and at that time some wag nicknamed it "Hide Park." In the year 1829 a group of Americans engaged in curing hides became homesick and longed for news from home. They discussed the matter and decided to make an American flag to use in signaling American ships which occasionally put in at San Diego Bay. Material for the flag proved difficult to find, but the problem was solved by collecting all of the red and blue calico and linen shirts of the American colony. From this material a passable reproduction of Old Glory was made, which was raised high over a hide warehouse, and the crew settled down again to the routine of the day. Historians have humorously suggested that California was thus brought into the Union without firearms.

35. POINT LOMA POST OFFICE, at Canyon Rd. junction, formerly known as Roseville, was settled about 1850 and named in honor of Louis Rose, a pioneer business man of San Diego. This small center is the principal Portuguese colony, members of which are engaged in tuna fishing. (See *Social and Cultural.*)

TOUR 3 — 4 *m.*
BALBOA PARK

The 1,400-acre tract of Balboa Park was established in 1868, but was not developed extensively until 1915, when the Panama-California Exposition was held. (See *The City by Sections: Balboa Park.*) This tour covers the developed section of the park.

E. from Fifth Ave. on Laurel St., which becomes El Prado.

El Prado runs through the park to the east entrance (Park Boulevard). On each side are Spanish Renaissance *palacios* (Sp., *palaces*), designed by the late Bertram Grosvenor Goodhue in 1915. They were restored and served in part for the exposition of 1935-6 and except as specially noted have been unused since. The buildings are designed with towers, colonnaded arcades, patios and ornate wall openings embellished with high relief ornament against cream-colored walls; the striking play of light and shade in the decorative scheme is especially effective in a country of intense sunlight.

36. The CABRILLO BRIDGE, crossed by *El Prado* (Sp., *the public walk*), is 450 feet long, and rises 110 feet above the canyon drive, in seven, tall, graceful cantilever arches. It is entirely of reinforced concrete construction, traversing a distance of 1500 feet of which 450 feet compose the bridge span, and was built from the plans of Frank P. Allen, architect, and Thomas B. Hunter, engineer. Below the bridge

(R) is the Laguna del Puente (Sp., *the lake of the bridge*), or LILY POOL, and from the bridge is a view of San Diego's main business district, the harbor, Point Loma, and the Coronado Islands.

37. EL PORTAL, at the extreme end of the bridge, is the west entrance to the exposition grounds and the group of buildings that lines El Prado. It bears the coat of arms of San Diego with two symbolic figures, in sculptured concrete, executed by Furio and Attilio Piccarilli, of New York.

38. The CALIFORNIA BUILDING AND QUADRANGLE (*open Tues.-Sat.*, 10-4:30; *Sun.* 1-4:30; *free*), a concrete building designed by Bertram Goodhue, includes the San Diego Museum, the Hall of Anthropology, the Franciscan Chapel, and the California Tower (*not open*). The Quadrangle, in the form of a Greek cross, has a dome embellished with a rich mosaic of highly glazed tile and surmounted by a lantern of rare beauty. The 200-foot tower is designed in three stages, the lower part relatively plain, pierced by small windows, and the upper part, forming the belfry, surmounted by a bell-shaped tile dome. The facade of the building is a fine example of Spanish Churrigueresque architecture with busts and statues of Spanish explorers and Franciscans who helped to make San Diego history incorporated in the design.

The SAN DIEGO MUSEUM AND ARCHEOLOGICAL INSTITUTE was organized in 1916 under the direction of Dr. Edgar L. Hewitt, director of the American School of Research, with the assistance of two directors of the Smithsonian Institution. Important exhibits are: the JESSOP COLLECTION OF ARCHERY; the MAYAN GALLERY, with plaster reproductions from Guatemala and Yucatan; pottery from Central and South America; weapons, stone carvings, ornaments, and basketry of southern Californian, Lower Californian, and South American Indians; and habitat groups of primitive Indians in life-size models. Murals by Cassidy and Vierra, in the great Hall of Archeology, depict various cliff dwellings and pueblo ruins of the Southwest. In the HALL OF ANTHROPOLOGY, which occupies the south side of the Quadrangle, is the permanent exhibit of the Smithsonian Institution's *History of Man*, in sculpture and clay.

L. from El Prado through first arcade.

39. A REPRODUCTION OF THE OLD GLOBE THEATER, (*private*), directly behind the California Building, was used in the exposition of 1935-36 for tabloid performances of Shakespeare. Because of the widespread interest in this theater, it is being made permanent to house a group of community players. The reproduction has been well done, and the grounds around the building are landscaped to represent a village green.

Retrace through arcade to El Prado; R. from El Prado at first opening.

40. The ALCAZAR GARDEN was formerly known as Montezuma's Garden, a name deriving from the exposition of 1915. Moorish fountains in blue, green, and yellow tile, pansy beds, and large blue jars mark this quiet retreat. An ornamental gateway on the south side of the garden opens onto a large lawn bowl surrounded by eucalyptus trees.

L. from gateway on gravel path to stone stairway.

41. PALM CANYON, crossed by a RUSTIC BRIDGE from the stairway, is a hidden canyon, literally crowded with palm trees. Over the tops of the palms (L) are visible corners of several *palacios* on El Prado, their

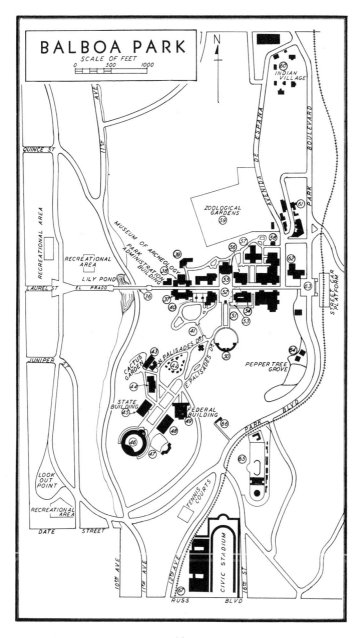

BALBOA PARK

SCALE OF FEET

0   500   1000

QUINCE ST

RECREATIONAL AREA

RECREATIONAL AREA

LAUREL ST

EL PRADO

LILY POND

JUNIPER ST

LOOK OUT POINT

RECREATIONAL AREA

DATE   STREET

INDIAN VILLAGE

ZOOLOGICAL GARDENS

MUSEUM OF ARCHEOLOGY

PARK ADMINISTRATION BUILDING

STREET CAR PLATFORM

AVENIDA DE ESPANA

PARK BOULEVARD

W. PALISADES DR.

E. PALISADES DR.

CACTUS GARDEN

PEPPER TREE GROVE

STATE BUILDING

FEDERAL BUILDING

PARK BLVD

TENNIS COURTS

CIVIC STADIUM

10TH AVE

11TH AVE

12TH AVE

16TH ST

RUSS   BLVD

85

creamy ornamented towers obscured by greenery. The far end of the bridge joins a stone stairway.

R. from bridge on trail; R. from trail on W. Palisades Dr.

42. The HOUSE OF PACIFIC RELATIONS (L) (*open; free*) is not in reality a single house but a group of small Spanish style buildings surrounding a large garden and pool. In these cottages the nations with interests in the Pacific Ocean area had headquarters during the exposition of 1935-36. At the far end (R) is the WISHING WELL which gathered many thousands of pennies during the two years of the Fair.

43. The PALACE OF EDUCATION (R) (*not open*) is a fine example of Spanish Pueblo architecture, a style developed in the colonial New Mexico area. This building will become a permanent museum for educational displays. At the south end of the building is a gravel path which goes to a CACTUS GARDEN in the rear.

44. The PALACE OF ENTERTAINMENT (R) (*private*), also in the Spanish Pueblo style, was used during the exposition of 1935-36 as a theater and dance hall. It is not in use.

45. The former STATE BUILDING (R) (*open*) houses the armory of the 251st Coast Artillery, Anti-Aircraft Corps, of the California National Guard. The building is of white stucco, of modified Spanish design.

46. The FORD BUILDING, end of the Palisades (*private*), is a circular, modern structure in white stucco with blue trim. This is a permanent addition to the park. It is proposed to make it a museum of mechanical progress and development.

W. Palisades Dr. circles and becomes E. Palisades Dr.

47. The FORD BOWL (R) (*open*) is an outdoor amphitheater named for Henry Ford, who took a great interest in the exposition of 1935-36. The bowl, built in a small ravine, is used for musical and outdoor entertainment. During the summer, regular concerts are given here by the San Diego Civic Symphony Orchestra. Free band concerts are given Sunday afternoons.

49. The FEDERAL BUILDING (R) (*private*) is a huge, windowless structure of concrete in the Mayan style, modeled from the Palace of the Governor at Uxmal, Yucatan. It is proposed to convert this building into a civic auditorium.

Palisades Dr. enters the Plaza de los Estados.

50. The SPRECKELS ORGAN PAVILION (R) (*open*) contains one of the world's largest outdoor organs, a gift to the city in 1915 by John D. and Adolph B. Spreckels. The building, of which Harrison Albright was the architect, consists of a great proscenium with somewhat flat gable ornamented with Plateresque detail. Curving around at the sides are walks in the form of a Corinthian peristyle, with an elaborate balustrade above. Organ concerts are given four afternoons each week, and many outdoor pageants and musical events appear on its stage.

51. The PLAZA DE LOS ESTADOS (Sp., *Square of the States*) is a long, flower-filled parkway in front of the organ pavilion. At the northern end of this plaza is the equestrian statue, *El Cid Campeador,* a boldly executed bronze sculpture by Anna Hyatt Huntington.

52. The PLAZA DE PANAMA is the great central plaza of the park. El Prado intersects this square, and the square is large enough to be used

LILY POND, BALBOA PARK, WITH EXPOSITION BUILDINGS
IN BACKGROUND *(Public Library photograph)*

as a parking place for automobiles of the Sunday afternoon crowds.

53. The CASA DEL REY MORO (Sp., *House of the Moorish King*) (R) (*open*) is used as a public cafe. Its balconies and terraced gardens, designed and planted in 1935 by Sam W. Hammil, San Diego architect, were modeled after a garden at Ronda, Spain. Under vine-covered pergolas bordered with close-clipped hedges and past gushing fountains, steps lead through the gradually falling terraces to the lowest level where a still pool mirrors an old well head amid the old-world charm of a Mediterranean garden.

54. The HOUSE OF HOSPITALITY, SE. cor. of El Prado and Plaza de Panama (*open*), was the reception hall for the exposition, but its rooms are now used as studios for artists and sculptors, and as meeting halls for clubs. Motion pictures and entertainments are given in the auditorium. The building is designed in a modified Plateresque style, has a corner tower, arcades, and projecting pavilions. The tower and windows are heavily ornamented and coats of arms of countries of the Pan-American Union are blazoned on the exterior walls. Massive arches, surmounted by more delicately designed Moorish arches on the balcony, surround the inner court which, with its boxwood hedges, border gardens, and palm trees, was designed in the manner of a convent patio in Guadalajara, Mexico. The centerpiece of the central fountain is the STATUE of a seated Mexican girl, the work of Donal Hord.

55. The FINE ARTS GALLERY OF SAN DIEGO, N. end of Plaza de Panama (*open, Mon. 10-4, 25c adm., Tues.-Sat., 10-4; Sun. 1-5; free*), is the only public art gallery in San Diego. This fine Spanish-

Renaissance building was completed in 1925 at a cost of $430,000, and was given to the city by Mr. and Mrs. Appleton S. Bridges. The general design of the imposing entrance facade of the building, based upon that of the University of Salamanca, Spain, has a great shell over the doorway honoring the memory of San Diego de Alcalá. The facade is further ornamented with statuary, relief busts, escutcheons, and an intricate medalion design. Except for the ornate windows of the first-story and the frieze which extends along the length of the building under the tiled eaves, the walls are otherwise unadorned. The interior is devoted to galleries of sculpture and painting, with smaller rooms containing laces, fabrics, glass, ceramics, dolls, ivories, oriental costumes, and other *objects d'art*. Four exceptional Flemish Renaissance tapestries are hung in the main halls. Panels of priceless laces and the great altarpiece, the Spanish *retablo* of St. John, are among the treasures of the gallery. The Arthur Putnam bronzes, a Japanese color-print collection, and the Carnegie collection of 18,000 art objects are displayed. The gallery possesses many fine paintings, some of the most outstanding being Zuloaga's full-length portrait of *Antonia La Gallega;* El Greco's *St. Francis;* two canvases by Zurbaran; a Murillo, a Rubens, and a Goya; and Sorolla's famous *Daughter María in the Gardens of La Granja,* which was the first gift to the Fine Arts Society. Among other works are examples of Henri, Chase, Matisse, Bellows, Corot, Courbet, and Fortuny.

Retrace the Plaza de Panama to El Prado; L. on El Prado.

56. The AMERICAN LEGION HEADQUARTERS, NE. cor. El Prado and the Plaza de Panama (*open*), was used as the Cafe of the World during the exposition. With its arcades and balconied windows the building suggests the richly ornamented urban palaces of Mexico, while the corner tower was modeled after that of the Palace of Monterey, at Salamanca, Spain.

57. The HORTICULTURAL BUILDING (L) is approached through the court called LA LAGUNA DE LAS FLORES (Sp., *Lake of the Flowers*), a lily pool with a myriad of goldfish. The Horticultural Building is a domed, lath house, open throughout the year, in which palms, tropical trees, flowers, and shrubs of semi-tropical varieties are seen. Of particular note are the many varieties of fern and begonias.

R. from the Horticultural Building on foot trail.

58. The JAPANESE PAVILION (*open*) is a charming Japanese house hidden in a bamboo grove. Designed in the manner of a Japanese temple by K. Tamia, a San Francisco architect, it is used as a tea garden. Japanese women in native costume prepare and serve Japanese foods. Stone lanterns from Nara, a winding stream with a vermillion BRIDGE OF LONG LIFE, and typical Japanese landscaping complete the isolated beauty of the spot.

L. from foot trail on Avenida de España (Sp., Avenue of Spain).

59. The ZOOLOGICAL GARDEN (L) (*open daily,* 8-5; *adm. adults,* 25c, *children under* 16, *free*), an outgrowth of the Panama-California Exposition of 1915, ranks as one of the four largest in America, and second in point of variety and rarity of specimen. Among the exhibits are the only mountain gorillas in captivity, captured in the Belgian Congo by the Martin Johnsons and given to the Zoo in 1931 by Miss Ellen

Scripps and Robert Scripps; California sea lions; the largest group of tortoises, and the largest specimen in captivity; the only California condor in captivity; sea elephants; a large collection of monkeys and parrots; and hundreds of other animals, in all 3,400 specimens. An animal amphitheater for trained seals, monkeys, and other animals, a modern arcaded reptile house, open dens for lions and tigers, and two enormous flying cages for birds, are among the many interesting points of the Zoo.

60. The INDIAN VILLAGE, at the end of La Avenida de España (*not open*), is used by the Boy Scouts for headquarters. It was built by the Santa Fe R. R. in 1915 for the Fair, and is a reproduction of the Pueblo of Taos, New Mexico.

Return on La Avenida de España.

61. The SPANISH VILLAGE (L) (*open daily; free*) is an art center, now housing Los Sureños Art Club and offering studios to individual artists. The quaint old-world cottages, in stucco and tile, are built haphazardly around an open patio.

62. The NATURAL HISTORY MUSEUM, NE. cor. of La Avenida de España and El Prado (*open daily 9-5; free*), is under the auspices of the San Diego Society of Natural History, which was incorporated in 1874. Three floors of exhibits are open to the public. The building, completed in 1933, is of reinforced concrete construction and Spanish colonial in design. Excepting the entrance facade, reached by a wide staircase leading to a platform before the doorway, the lower floors are devoid of ornamentation. The arched windows with carved balusters in the top-story and the frieze which extends over the slightly overhanging cornice, relieve the plainness of the walls below. The ground floor, reached from the Avenida, houses the SCIENTIFIC LIBRARY, as well as the museum laboratories, and also contains dinosaur fossil, mineral, reptile, and fish exhibits. On the main floor is the Stephens collection of birds and mammals, mounted in cabinets, as habitat groups. The Ingersoll collection of bird's eggs and nests occupies cabinets along the walls. The top floor exhibits cover sea shells, corals, fossils, butterflies, and insects, including live black widow spiders and a collection of 1,200 water-color flower portraits presented by Ellen B. Scripps.

63. PEPPER TREE GROVE, an outdoor picnic ground (*open; free*), is reached by a driveway which runs S. from El Prado, directly across from the Natural History Museum. Various clubs and state societies meet here.

64. Park Boulevard is the east entrance to the improved section of the park area. Across the street from the end of El Prado is the ARCADED WAITING PLATFORM for the Nos. 7 and 11 streetcars. To the R. paralleling the street is a footpath that skirts the edge of this area.

R. on Park Blvd.

Pepper Tree Grove (see above), lies R. about one block beyond El Prado.

65. The NAVAL HOSPITAL (L) is on an elevated mesa occupying 38 acres originally a part of Balboa Park. The city of San Diego conveyed 22.5 acres to the United States Government in 1919 and the additional acreage was granted in 1937. The buildings, of Spanish-Moorish design, were begun in 1920 from plans drawn by Naval architects in Washington, and the hospital was commissioned in 1922. There are now more

than 30 units in the group. The ADMINISTRATION BUILDING, four stories in height, with a tower consisting of two more stories, has a patio to the rear around which other buildings are grouped. Mr. William H. Crofts, master gardener for ten years of the Duke of Norfolk's estate in England, and with years of experience in America, developed the excellent landscaping of the area. The institution provides free hospitalization for men active in the Army and Navy, for those retired in good standing, and for the families of both groups. A staff of 50 doctors, 60 nurses, 7 dentists, and a corps of 250 takes care of between 800 and 1,000 patients daily.

66. A PUBLIC RIDING ACADEMY (R) has its stables here. Expert horsemen teach beginners in the ring adjoining the stables.

67. The SAN DIEGO SENIOR HIGH SCHOOL (L), at the NE. cor. of Russ and Park Boulevard, is a group of ivy-covered buildings constructed of gray stone and concrete. The CITY STADIUM is directly behind the school and faces on Russ Boulevard. It was built for the 1915 fair and has a seating capacity of 60,000 people. The SNYDER CONTINUATION SCHOOL (R) furnishes a complete curriculum from kindergarten to college courses.

Russ Boulevard is the end of the park area.

TOUR 4 — 2.5 m.

THE WATERFRONT

This tour covers San Diego's colorful waterfront, described in Max Miller's novel, *I Cover the Waterfront.*

S. from Vine St. on Pacific Hwy.

68. The CONSOLIDATED AIRCRAFT CORPORATION, 3302 Pacific Hwy. (*private*), employs 3,250 skilled workmen and constructs 100 to 150 airplanes a year. The buildings are of modern design, with saw-tooth-type roof set with windows facing the north to prevent glare, which might disturb aviators landing on nearby Lindbergh Field.

69. The RYAN AERONAUTICAL COMPANY, S. of the Consolidated plant (*private*), was formerly the Ryan Airlines, which built the *Spirit of St. Louis* for Col. Charles A. Lindbergh. The RYAN SCHOOL OF AERONAUTICS, in connection with the company, has 135 students enrolled.

70. LINDBERGH FIELD, the municipal airport (R), contains 287 acres, dredged from the bay in 1930. Sixty-two acres are surfaced to facilitate landings and take-offs. There is a seaplane anchorage with ramps at the south end of the field. The UNITED AIRLINES DEPOT (L) is a combination hangar, office building, and waiting room. The ADMINISTRATION BUILDING, of Spanish design surrounded by palm trees and gardens, which stands in the center of the airport buildings, is a depot for the Western Air Express, and houses the offices of the United States Customs, the Weather Bureau, and the Lindbergh Field Cafe.

71. The UNITED STATES ARMY AIR CORPS HANGARS (L), two in number, are at the end of Lindbergh Field.

R. from Pacific Hwy. on Laurel St.; L. from Laurel St. on Belt St.

WATERFRONT FROM THE AIR
(Official U. S. Navy photograph)

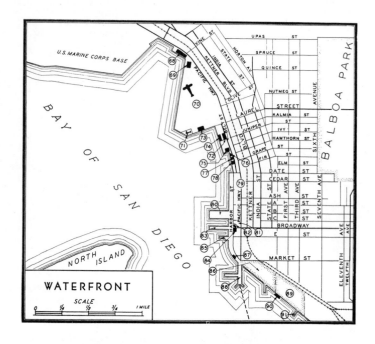

WATERFRONT

SCALE

72. A SEAFOOD CANNING COMPANY (R), foot of Juniper St. (*open when in operation*), ships hundreds of carloads of tuna, mackerel, and sardines annually, 90 percent going to eastern markets. This plant employs 350 men and women during the fishing season. Nearly 50 fishing boats unload regularly at the company docks, bringing their cargo from Mexican waters, 500 to 3,000 miles away. Behind this cannery a road passes the fishing docks. The rocks along the shore are covered with fish scales so deeply that they appear to be covered with snow.

73. The UNITED STATES COAST GUARD STATION, on the road behind the cannery (R), has a large seaplane hangar, a cement runway extending into the bay, and two barracks of Spanish design with messrooms and quarters to accommodate 40 men.

Retrace to Belt St.; R. on Belt St. to Juniper St.

74. The SOLAR AIRCRAFT COMPANY (R), 1212 Juniper St. (*private*), makes and ships airplane parts, specializing in manifolds for which it has an international reputation. Beginning in 1930 with half a dozen men, this company has achieved such recognition for its excellent workmanship that more than one hundred workmen are now employed. In this building the *Spirit of St. Louis* was constructed in 1927. A MARKER in commemoration of this event has been placed in front of the SE. corner of the building.

Retrace Juniper St.; R. on Belt St.

75. The HEADQUARTERS OF THE 1ST BATTALION, United

States Naval Reserves, 2162 Belt St. (*open*), is at the rear of a deserted cannery building. It has offices, a school for the Naval Reserves, an armory, and a drill floor.

76. The CANNERY INSPECTION DIVISION of the California Department of Public Health, 2160 Belt St., has offices in a temporary wooden structure. This is the home office for the inspectors, who are stationed at each of San Diego's five canneries to inspect the fish at every stage of the canning process. Boats and docks for the Naval Reserve Headquarters are behind this building. A dozen small piers are seen, to which scores of fishing boats, sailboats, and small yachts are tied. This small bay will be filled in and all buildings between this point and the airfield will be removed by 1942, when the cannery leases expire.

77. A STEEL BOAT, 2110 Belt St., flat-bottomed with steel top, lies a few feet out of the water, near a quaint English style building used as a cafe. The boat does not appear high enough for a man to stand upright, yet it has been occupied for years by a beachcomber, who without much urging will weave tales for the passer-by. Built in this strange shape as an experimental lifeboat, it was brought to San Diego from Panama.

78. The SOUTHWESTERN YACHT CLUB (R), foot of Grape St. (*open*), has approximately 75 members and 40 boats. Behind the clubhouse are the yacht club wharves. In the vicinity of the club are many boatbuilding and repair concerns. Numerous boats are drydocked here, and a fishing boat is usually in the process of construction.

R. from Belt St. on Date St.; L. from Date St. on Harbor St.

79. The CIVIC CENTER (L) when completed will extend from Grape to Ash Streets. The grounds will be landscaped and Harbor Street, the present bayfront boulevard, will be extended around the rim of the bay to the yacht basin at La Playa on Point Loma, almost directly opposite.

ARCHITECT'S SKETCH OF THE CIVIC CENTER

93

Beyond the Civic Center are Navy boats, Coast Guard cutters and tankers tied to mooring bitts alongside the embarcadero.

80. MUNICIPAL PIER NO. 1 (R), foot of B St., is nearly a fifth of a mile in length and unusually wide. It is occupied by a warehouse, the offices of shipping companies, and the HIRING HALL of the International Longshoremen's and Warehousemen's Union. The waterfront from this point is lined with palm trees.

81. The LANE BASEBALL FIELD (L), NE. cor. Harbor St. and Broadway, is the home grounds of the San Diego Padres, a team of the Pacific Coast League, which won the coast pennant in 1937.

82. The HARBOR DEPARTMENT BUILDING (L), NE. cor. Harbor St. and Broadway, is triangular in shape and houses the executive offices of the San Diego Harbor Department.

83. BROADWAY PIER (municipal) (R), foot of Broadway, houses offices of STATE and FEDERAL RELIEF AGENCIES, STEAMSHIP COMPANIES, the MEXICAN INTERNATIONAL FISHING DIVISION, CALIFORNIA DIVISION OF FISH AND GAME, COMMERCIAL LICENSES, and the DEEP SEA AND PURSE SEINE FISHERMEN'S UNION, besides warehouses for steamship freight. On each side of Broadway pier are small wharves for sport fishing boats, Navy shore boats, water taxis, and vessels plying between North Island and the mainland.

84. HEADQUARTERS OF THE ELEVENTH NAVAL DISTRICT (L), SE. corner of Broadway and Harbor St., is a six-story building which also contains the Naval commissary supply depct.

85. NAVY PIER (R), foot of E St., has a provision and inspection depot at the entrance. Naval supplies are unloaded here from trucks and are picked up by Navy boats.

Beyond Navy pier, along the bay line, are the offices of the MEXICAN GOVERNMENT FISHING INSPECTION; commercial SPORT FISHING COMPANIES; the SCHOOL AND OFFICE of a licensed master mariner; and a NOVELTY SHOP whose main income is derived from selling souvenirs to sailors and tourists.

86. BATTERY PARK, between Market St. and U. S. Bulkhead line; E. from shoreline to Navy Field, is now being reconstructed and developed by the city. FISHERMEN'S WHARF, foot of F St., has numerous fishing enterprises clustered on it. DEAD MEN'S POINT (Sp., *Punta de los Muertos*), foot of Market Street, was originally a sandspit, on which a number of sailors and marines from the crews of two ships, members of a Spanish squadron, were buried in 1787. They died while surveying the bay area. A MARKER has been placed near the site of the old burial ground.

87. The HALL OF THE INTERNATIONAL LONGSHOREMEN'S AND WAREHOUSEMEN'S UNION (R) was the scene of much activity during the waterfront strikes of 1934 and 1936.

88. The CORONADO FERRY SLIP (R), foot of Pacific Hwy., is the ferry depot for transportation of passengers and automobiles to Coronado.
L. from Harbor St. on Market St.; R. from Market St. on Union St.

89. NAVY FIELD, on waterfront bet. Union St. and Fifth Ave., is a baseball park and recreational grounds for the Navy personnel. Soccer games are sometimes scheduled here.

90. The STAR OF INDIA (R), foot of First Ave. (*open; adm.* 10c), is an all-iron boat built in England in 1863. It was an immigrant ship in use for 30 years between England and New Zealand, and is the last full-rigged iron ship afloat. It is owned by the Zoological Society of San Diego, which operates it as a museum.

91. The SAN DIEGO ROWING CLUB, foot of Fifth Ave., was established in 1883. Navy boats and water taxis dock at the small pier. The island to the L. of the pier, with house and bamboo fence, was built as a windbreak to facilitate the landing of shore boats.

TOUR 5 — 24.1 *m.*

BEACH TOWNS

SW. From Voltaire St. on Bacon St.

92. OCEAN BEACH (20 alt., 4,012 pop.), is a residential and resort area which offers beach sports and recreational facilities, including an indoor salt-water plunge (*open all year; reasonable prices*). Accommodations are adequate. Along the shore of Mission Bay, at the northern limits of this settlement, is a State fish and game refuge. This region is a mating place for seafowl, and is the habitat of fiddler crabs, scallops, and various species of clams.

L. from Bacon St. on Coronado St.; R. from Coronado St. on Sunset Cliffs Blvd.

SUNSET CLIFFS is a distinctive suburb of Ocean Beach. Rustic bridges, shelters, and stairways have been built along the rugged sea cliffs.

Retrace Sunset Cliffs Blvd. to Coronado St.; L. on Coronado St. to Bacon St.; R. on Bacon St. to W. Point Loma Blvd.; L. on W. Point Loma Blvd. to Mission Blvd.; R. on Mission Blvd.

93. MISSION BAY (R), formerly known as False Bay, is eight square miles of shallow water spanned by a bridge which crosses the narrow channel. Fishing from the bridge is permitted.

94. MISSION BEACH, (25 alt., 1,092 pop.), is the trading center for the beach resort and residential area on Medanos (Sp., *dunes*) Point. Along the strand are facilities for surf and bay fishing, bathing, rowing, and yachting. There is a grammar school for this district, but high school students must go to either La Jolla or Point Loma High School.

95. PACIFIC BEACH, (65 alt., 1,626 pop.), on the slopes of the La Jolla promontory, began as a small farming district, but water shortage retarded its development. At present it is entirely a home and resort suburb. There is a section of this beach exclusively for Negroes.

L. from Mission Blvd. on Garnet St.

The BEACH PIER (*open, free; small charge for fishing privileges*), is privately owned.

Retrace Garnet St. to Mission Blvd.; L. on Mission Blvd. to Turquoise St.; L. on Turquoise St. which becomes La Jolla Blvd. which becomes Prospect Ave.

96. LA JOLLA (0 to 800 alt., 5,000 pop.), is a residential community on the western slope of Mount Soledad (822 alt.). The name is com-

monly supposed to be derived from the Spanish *La Joya* (*the jewel*), but there is evidence that it may have been derived from an Indian word meaning "hidden caves." All accommodations, including apartments and American and European plan hotels, are available. Recreational facilities include an 18-hole golf course, completely grassed, on the slope of Mount Soledad; riding academies; aquaplaning; beach bathing; tennis; and yachting. Annual sport events are the La Jolla Ruff Water Swimming Race, held in August, and the tennis tournament held in July at the community playgrounds. La Jolla is the home of a number of writers, among whom are Walt Mason, Max Miller, and Walt Coburn. Artists frequently exhibit their works at the art gallery in the public library, Girard and Wall Streets. Outstanding in the growth and development of La Jolla was Ellen Browning Scripps of the well-known newspaper publishing family. She donated the money and in some instances the land to build many of the scientific, cultural and recreational enterprises in the town. Her gifts to La Jolla include: THE SCRIPPS INSTITUTION OF OCEANOGRAPHY (1911-1920), The LA JOLLA WOMAN'S CLUB (1904), the playgrounds and community houses (1915), BISHOP'S SCHOOL (1916), the sanitarium (1918), the LA JOLLA LIBRARY (1921), the hospital and clinic (1924), the nurses' home (1925), and the children's pool (1931). Miss Scripps died in 1932 at the age of 90, and in her will provided funds for the maintenance of her favorite institutions. In the La Jolla area two deposits of archeological remains provide evidence of a prehistoric race which existed along the coast 5,000 or more years ago. In the fairly recent past, La Jolla was a summer camping ground of back country Indian hill tribes.

97. SCRIPPS MEMORIAL HOSPITAL AND METABOLIC CLINIC, 464-476 Prospect Avenue (*private*), was built in 1924-1928. This is one of the few clinics in the United States doing research work on the process of metabolism. The hospital, which has facilities for 27 patients, in addition to accepting general cases, is equipped with electrocardiograph metabolar machines, special diet kitchens and research laboratories.

98. BISHOP'S SCHOOL, 475 Prospect Avenue (*private*), is an Episcopalian school for girls, built with funds donated by Ellen Browning Scripps. The tiled chapel tower won the architect, Carleton Winslow, a certificate of honor from the American Institute of Architects.

L. from Prospect Ave. on Girard St.; R. from Girard St. on Coast Blvd.

99. The LA JOLLA CAVES (*open; adm.* 25c), are mentioned in the *Encyclopedia Americana* as one of the most interesting sights in southern California. Originally the seven caves could be reached only from the water, but about 1905 a German professor, Gustav Schultz, cut a land entrance to the largest of the caves. Geologists say that this is the only cave, with the exception of Fingal's Cave in Scotland, which has its peculiar stratification.

L. from Coast Blvd. on Prospect Ave.; L. from Prospect Ave. on Torrey Pine Rd. to La Jolla Shores Dr.; L. on La Jolla Shores Dr.

100. SCRIPPS INSTITUTION OF OCEANOGRAPHY (*open; free*), is under the supervision of the Regents of the University of California. The institution, highly departmentalized, is devoted to the scientific study

COASTLINE NORTH OF LA JOLLA
(Johnson photograph)

CORONADO FROM THE AIR, WITH HOTEL DEL
CORONADO IN FOREGROUND *(Hotel del Coronado photograph)*

of marine life, ocean temperatures and currents, fish and biology, and other subjects pertaining to the ocean. The scientific staff consists of about 20 members. Physical equipment includes two laboratory buildings and the SCRIPPS INSTITUTION PIER (*open daily; fishing permitted*). *Retrace La Jolla Shores Dr. to Torrey Pine Rd.; L. on Torrey Pine Road.*

101. TORREY PINES MESA, junction US 101, was named for the famous Torrey pines which grow on rock-buttressed slopes overlooking the ocean. These grotesque, wind-blown trees, said to be found in only one other location in the world, were discovered and named in 1850 by Dr. C. C. Parry, botanist of the International Boundary Survey.

TOURS IN ENVIRONS

TOUR 6

CORONADO—OLD MEXICO

San Diego—San Ysidro—Tijuana—Ensenada—Coronado—San Diego.
US 101, Mexican National Highway, Silver Strand Drive, Coronado
Ferry.
San Diego to Ensenada and return, 173.5 *m.*
Route paralleled by San Diego and Arizona Eastern R. R. between San
Diego and Mexican border.
Usual accommodations; service stations at infrequent intervals S. of
Mexican border.
American citizens going only as far S. as Ensenada may enter Mexico by
calling at the Mexican Immigration Office in Tijuana, Mexico, and stating purpose of trip. Tourists of other nationalities should see Mexican
Consul at San Diego.

CAUTION: Drive slowly over Mexican National Highway, especially
on curves where visibility is reduced and where slow-moving horsemen,
cattle, or wagons are likely to be encountered.

From sea level at San Diego, the route goes SE. through a thickly
settled area, skirts San Diego Bay, and crosses the international boundary
line at a point about 6 miles from the sea. From Tijuana the route goes
to the seacoast and parallels the beach almost the entire way to Ensenada,
with occasional detours into the hills and valleys, which are typical of
the northern section of Baja California.

From Fifth Ave. and Broadway in downtown San Diego, 0 *m.*, the
route goes E. on Broadway to Twelfth Ave., R. on Twelfth Ave. to Main
St. (US 101), and L. on US 101.

At 3.9 *m.* is the junction with Thirty-second Ave.

> Right on this street to the UNITED STATES DESTROYER BASE,
> 1 *m.* (*open Sat. and Sun.,* 1-4 *p. m.*). At the Destroyer Base light
> craft and submarines of the United States Navy are decommissioned,
> recommissioned, repaired, and docked. It is also the home station
> of the U. S. S. *Rigel,* tender for the decommissioned destroyers, as
> well as receiving ship for the Eleventh Naval District. The station
> consists of 42 buildings, with machine shops equipped to repair any
> type of naval vessel. Attached permanently to the base are 40 naval
> officers and 350 men and a Marine detachment of 100 men. Of
> particular interest are the traveling crane (visible from US 101)
> and the *Ard-1,* the Navy's first mobile floating drydock.

NATIONAL CITY, 4.5 *m.* (50 alt., 7,301 pop.), adjoins the southern city limits of San Diego. This residential city is in the rich agricultural area formerly known as the *Rancho de la Nacion* (Sp., *ranch of the
nation*), which was administered by the *comandante* of the presidio at
Old Town in the name of the Spanish crown. It became state land during the Mexican regime; 6 leagues of it were granted in 1845 to Don

Juan Forster, an American who became a naturalized Mexican.

Between National City and San Ysidro, the route goes through one of the foremost celery producing districts in the United States and traverses a section of citrus groves, bordered by stately eucalyptus trees. At 8 *m.* is the junction with a paved road.

> Left on this road is CHULA VISTA (Sp., *pretty view*), 0.5 *m.* (175 alt., 4,500 pop.), center of a farming district known as the South Bay Region.

SAN YSIDRO (Sp., *St. Isidore*), 15.5 *m.* (70 alt.), is one of the principal United States ports of entry for southern California, frequently called the Gateway to Old Mexico.

The INTERNATIONAL BOUNDARY LINE between the United States and Mexico, 16 *m.,* marks the end of US 101. Offices of the United States Customs, Immigration, Agricultural Inspection, and Public Services are in the buildings to the left of the gateway.

Persons returning to the United States from Mexico must make a declaration to the customs officers covering all goods and merchandise. Articles for personal or household use, up to the value of $100, are exempt from import duty. This exemption is allowed each person not oftener than every 30 days. Cigars, cigarettes, tobacco, and foodstuffs may be included with the exemption, but the quantities are limited. American citizens wishing to visit any place farther S. than Ensenada, or in the interior of Mexico, must obtain a tourist card (*cost* $1.01 *in U. S. currency*) from the nearest Mexican Consul, or from the Mexican Immigration Office at the port of entry.

TIJUANA (probably a Spanish corruption of the Indian word *Tiwana, by the sea*), 17 *m.* (25 alt., 11,271 pop.), is reached by a long, narrow wooden bridge spanning the Tijuana River. The frequently used name, "Tia Juana" (Sp., *Aunt Jane*), is a further corruption of the original. Though this border resort has lost much of its attraction since the legalization of liquor in the United States and the ban on gambling enforced by the Mexican Government in 1935, it continues to interest tourists and nearby residents. The main street is lined with saloons and places of amusement, usually well patronized. Curio stores feature Mexican and imported articles, and small boys are everywhere selling Mexican cigarettes. Because the town is a free-zone port, European goods may be bought on which no import duty has been paid.

South of Tijuana the paved Mexican National Highway goes out of the valley and down a series of winding grades to the seashore. At 18.6 *m.* is a junction with a paved road.

> Left on this road is AGUA CALIENTE (Sp., *hot water*), 1 *m.,* a border resort opened in 1928, featuring mineral springs of claimed medicinal value. Within a few years a $10,000,000 plant was built for gambling and racing, but the decree of President Lazaro Cardenas, in July 1935, banning gambling throughout Mexico, sounded the apparent death knell of this famous spa. In the spring of 1937, however, Agua Caliente reopened, without gambling, but with legalized horse racing, then closed again in September because of wage disputes.

SHORE ACRES, 33.2 *m.,* is an eating place and former country club, now operated as a fashionable seaside hotel and resort. Murals depict the origin of the Mexican people. Hunting, fishing, and swimming facilities are available.

Between Shore Acres and Ensenada the road traverses a rugged wind-blown wilderness. (*A careful check should be kept on water, oil, and gas, because of the distance between stations. Telephone service to Tijuana and the United States is available at most of the resorts.*) The route constantly touches the ocean, hovers briefly, and returns inland over tortuous grades and curves. Mountains which appear copper- and brown-hued nearby become turquoise at a distance. TABLE MT., a huge, flat-topped mesa (L) is visible for miles.

ROSARITO BEACH, 33.6 *m.*, is a service station and eating place, with cabin, hunting, fishing, and swimming facilities.

DESCANSO (Sp., *rest*), 47.6 *m.*, is a beach resort, with restaurant, filling station, and facilities for fishing and riding.

The HALFWAY HOUSE, 49 *m.*, overlooks the rock-buttressed coast line. Here are refreshments, gas, and oil, and cabin, fishing, and hunting facilities. Most of this quiet, rugged landscape was originally part of old Spanish land grants, and at present is divided into ranches. A few gold mines are operated in the district, but for the most part the territory is only partially explored.

LA MISION (Sp., *the mission*), 58 *m.*, is a service station with restaurant and hotel. The CLUB CAZADORES (Sp., *hunters' club*) is located here.

JATAY, 62 *m.*, is a roadside service station, with cabins for rent along the seashore. (*Between Jatay and Ensenada there is no opportunity to refuel or obtain water.*)

At 79.5 *m.* is a junction with a dirt road.

> Left on this road is GUADALUPE, 16 *m.*, a Russian colony. The holdings of this colony are community owned, and all transactions are made on a cooperative basis. San Antonio, a sister colony, is 4 miles S. of Guadalupe. The community was established in 1906. Wheat, the chief crop, is milled into flour at Ensenada. Members of the colony call themselves All-Believers, are forbidden to shave, do not eat pork, and observe Saturday as the Sabbath.

ENSENADA (Sp., *cove*), 86 *m.*, sprawls along the beach in the curve of TODOS SANTOS (Sp., *all saints*) BAY. (*All accommodations.*) Ensenada's climate is considered almost ideal. In the bay and around Todos Santos Islands are tuna, swordfish, yellowtail, barracuda, and bonita. Fresh bay lobster, wild game, and fowl are almost daily items on Ensenada menus. Here is a palatial hotel and resort, planned in part by Jack Dempsey.

Return by the same route to San Ysidro, 156 *m.*. L. from San Ysidro on National Ave.

At PALM CITY, 161 *m.*, the route goes L.

IMPERIAL BEACH, 163.6 *m.*, is a seaside resort.

The route follows the SILVER STRAND, a narrow strip of sandy beach separating San Diego Bay from the ocean.

TENT CITY, at the N. end of Silver Strand Drive, is a 24-acre section of the strand that has been converted into a resort area. It extends for half a mile along the narrow sandspit and has an amusement center with a casino, pool hall, and dance hall. (*Cottages and tent houses rent at reasonable rates by the day, week, or month.*)

CORONADO, 171.5 *m.* (25 alt., 5,412 pop.), a noted residential and resort community northwest of the Silver Strand, was named for the Coronado Islands, which lie to the S. in Mexican waters. It is an incorporated city, operating under a city-manager plan. The population has a large proportion of service men, many of whom are retired and living on pension.

At 171.5 *m.* is the junction with Orange Ave.

At the head of Orange Ave. is the HOTEL DEL CORONADO, opened in 1888 as "the largest hotel in the world." (See illus. p. 97.) Stanford White, New York architect, designed the rambling building, a distinctive feature of which is its towers. The hotel, in a 7½-acre tropical garden, has housed chief executives of the United States and continues to serve the socially prominent of all nations. Social life centers around the yacht club, the country club, and the various clubs of the service men. During summer months Saturday night dances are well attended. The annual tennis and golf tournament and horse show are usually scenes of social festivity.

At 172.5 *m.* is a junction with Fourth St.

Left on Fourth St. to a bridge connecting Coronado with NORTH ISLAND, on the end of the peninsula, one of the United States' greatest air bases. All cars are stopped at the far end of the bridge by the Marine guard, and entrance to the area is permitted after car inspection. (*No cameras or sketching allowed on government property.*)

ROCKWELL FIELD (L) is the main landing field; the various buildings house water and land planes, lighter-than-air craft, service shops, and the homes and living quarters of the officers and enlisted men. Carrier craft are anchored along the bayshore of the island between cruises.

The route follows Orange Ave. to the CORONADO FERRY SLIP (for rates see *General Information: Transportation*).

From the ferry slip, at the foot of Market St. in San Diego, the route goes E. on Market St. to Fifth Ave. and L. on Fifth Ave. to Broadway, 173.5 *m.*

TOUR 7

OLD MISSIONS

San Diego—Encinitas—Oceanside—San Luis Rey Mission—Escondido—San Diego Mission—San Diego.
US 101, Mission Road, US 395.
San Diego to San Diego, 103.2 *m.*
Route paralleled by Santa Fe R. R. between San Diego and Oceanside.
Adequate accommodations, including trailer camps.
Paved roads throughout, open all seasons.

CAUTION: It is advisable to swim only at established centers where lifeguards are on duty. Hunting of small game and deer is permissible in season along the route, except in certain signposted areas.

This route goes northwest along the coast line and through the San Luis Rey River valley; returning it climbs to a highland valley, swings southwest, and descends to the California shore across Kearny Mesa. The scenery varies from ocean surf and sea cliffs to mountain valleys and inland plateaus.

From San Diego, 0 *m.*, the route goes W. on Broadway to Pacific Hwy. (US 101) ; R. on Pacific Hwy.

At 12 *m.* is a junction with Torrey Pines Rd. (see *Tour* 5).

Left on this road to La Jolla, 3 *m.*

TORREY PINES PARK, 15 *m.*, on Torrey Pines Mesa, sets aside and preserves the few remaining Torrey pines, said to grow in only one other place in the world. These grotesque, wind-blown trees were discovered and named in the spring of 1850 by Dr. C. C. Parry, botanist of the International Boundary Survey.

DEL MAR (Sp., *of the sea*), 17.5 *m.* (100 alt., 500 pop.), a beach residential town, is the scene of San Diego's annual County Fair held in the late summer.

At 18 *m.* is a junction with a paved road.

Right on this road to the SAN DIEGO COUNTY FAIRGROUNDS AND RACE TRACK, 1 *m.* The grounds are under the supervision of the Twenty-second Agricultural District of California. Bing Crosby, film and radio star, is president of the Del Mar Turf Club. During the first racing season, 22 days in July of 1937, the Del Mar Track became an important adjunct to the sporting and recreational facilities of California.

SOLANA BEACH (Sp., *sunny place*), 20 *m.* (10 to 100 alt., 550 pop.), offers camping, surf bathing, and fishing (*cottages available; rates reasonable*). Several small farms in this vicinity are devoted to citrus fruit, avocado, flower, and bulb raising.

At 20 *m.* is a junction with the Rancho Santa Fe Rd.

Right on this road to RANCHO SANTA FE, 5.4 *m.* (200 alt., 800 pop.), founded in 1922 by the Santa Fe R. R. This was originally the San Dieguito Rancho, which the company bought in 1906; making experimental plantings of eucalyptus trees to be used for railroad ties. In 1927 the railroad company sold the tract to a group of southern California capitalists, who developed the property into an exclusive residential and farming district. Citrus fruits and avocados are the principal products. Douglas Fairbanks, Sr., owns a 3,000-acre ranch here, and Bing Crosby maintains a country estate. A portion of the original adobe *casa de la hacienda* (Sp., *main ranch house*) of Juan Maria Osuna, who was San Diego's first mayor in 1835, has been incorporated in the mansion built by Crosby.

CARDIFF, 22 *m.* (100 alt., 100 pop.), is a block (R) from the highway. The few stores of the business district are built in mission style.

ENCINITAS (Sp., *little live oaks*), 24 *m.*, yields nearly $1,000,000 yearly in blossoms and bulbs, which are shipped in refrigerator cars directly to the eastern markets. The National Midwinter Flower Show is held here during the month of February. Encinitas was settled in 1854 by a group of Germans from Chicago.

At 26 *m.* the highway passes between two rows of huge eucalyptus trees, and is separated into two lanes by a central row of these trees.

CARLSBAD, 33 *m.* (50 alt., 1,660 pop.) (*excellent hotel and road-*

house accommodations). In 1887 mineral springs were discovered here, and were found to have practically the same chemical content as the famous mineral springs at Karlsbad in Europe. During the World War the name was cut to Carl, but later was restored to Carlsbad. The surrounding region is noted for its production of winter vegetables, flowers, bulbs, and citrus fruits.

OCEANSIDE, 36.5 *m.* (300 alt., 4,500 pop.), is a residential town, beach resort, and agricultural distribution point of importance to the county. (*Beach camp sites and cottages available.*) A charge is made for the use of the MUNICIPAL CAMPGROUND, near the mouth of the San Luis Rey (Sp., *St. Louis, King*) River. On the beach, beneath the pier, is a MUNICIPAL DINING ROOM (*open, free; gas stoves, tables, benches*). The pier, extending 1,700 ft. into the ocean, is equipped for fishing and for docking small boats.

The bulb and flower growing industry of San Diego County is centralized in the Oceanside-Carlsbad area. Along the highway on the outskirts of the city are several commercial gardens.

At 36.5 *m.* is a junction with Mission Road; R. on Mission Road.

At 37.5 *m.* are the grounds and buildings of the ROSICRUCIAN FELLOWSHIP (L), world center of Rosicrucian philosophy, established in 1911 by Max Heindel. East from this point the route goes up the SAN LUIS REY VALLEY, a rich horticultural, agricultural, and citrus-producing district. In common with other southern California rivers, the San Luis Rey (L) is usually dry for several miles inland from the sea during the summer months. In the middle distance to the E. is PALOMAR MOUNTAIN; NE. are the snowcapped peaks of the SAN JACINTO and SAN BERNARDINO ranges.

SAN LUIS REY MISSION, 41.6 *m.* (*open; donation customary*) presents an impressive picture with its long facade, two-storied campanile, and the high wall of El Campo Santo (Sp., *the cemetery*). It stands on an eminence which overlooks the surrounding country. Sections of a great adobe wall which once encircled the buildings and garden lands still remain. Brothers of the order in attendance escort visitors over the grounds and explain the plan of the building and its history.

Founded in June, 1798, and named *La Mision de San Luis Rey de Francia* (Sp., *The Mission of St. Louis, King of France*), it became the greatest of the mission establishments. Like all the missions founded by Father Serra, it is in a fertile area which supported a large Indian population, and its location was chosen so travelers of the time could make it a stop-over station, a one-day horseback ride from either Mission San Diego to the south, or from Mission San Juan Capistrano to the north.

This mission was the work of two untiring priests, Fr. Juan Norberto de Santiago and Fr. Antonio Peyri, who spent 34 years among the Luiseño Indians. By 1827 the mission owned 22,610 head of cattle, 27,412 sheep, 1,120 goats, 280 hogs, 1,501 horses, and 235 mules.

The foundations of the present church were laid in 1811, and dedication services were performed on Oct. 4, 1815, the feast day of St. Francis. Architecturally this mission is the most perfect of all the California missions. A composite of Spanish, Moorish, and Mexican, its architecture has been rightly called Mission. The buildings covered an area of more than six acres, and the facade of the mission was 600 ft. long. The present restoration has preserved admirably the Indian mural decorations of the chapel.

In the oval space over the arch spanning the entrance to the mortuary chapel is the emblem of the Third Order of St. Francis—a cross and the Stigmata (Five Wounds) of Christ. Eight massive columns support the ceiling and brick dome high over the altar, the rear wall of which is decorated in the classic manner. Low, open doorways on both sides of the altar lead to stairs to a tower used in olden days by "watchers of the dead." In the cemetery is a wooden cross said to be the one used when the mission was founded.

At 44.5 *m.* is a junction with an oiled road.

Right on this road to the OLD ADOBE HOUSE of the RANCHO GUAJOME (Ind., *home of the frog*), 2.5 *m.* This house (*open to public by special permission from the resident owner*) was built in 1853 by Lieut. Cave J. Couts. Four long wings, containing 20 rooms, surround a patio, or central garden space, which is 80 by 90 ft. The roofs are still covered with the original dull-red tiles said to have been molded over the legs of Indian neophytes at Mission San Luis Rey. Cave J. Couts, Jr., who inherited the property, maintains it in the style of a Mexican hacienda, and employs Indian servants. Mr. Couts sleeps in the same room and bed in which he was born. Helen Hunt Jackson visited *Guajome* (pronounced, wah-home-aye) and described the rancho in her novel, *Ramona.*

At 46.4 *m.* is a junction with US 395 (see *Tour 7A*), at a concrete bridge spanning the San Luis Rey River. The route goes R. on US 395 over rolling hills planted with avocado, citrus, and other fruit trees. This region is divided into small orchard ranches, usually of only a few acres each, on which the owners live.

VISTA, 51 *m.* (330 alt., 544 pop.), has a small business district. When the Oceanside-Escondido branch of the Santa Fe R. R. was completed in 1890, a post office and store were established at this site. In 1926, water was brought to the district from Lake Henshaw, 40 miles away, and the town development began. Though a recent town, Vista possesses one of the oldest wineries in southern California, and the whole district traces its history to the old Buena Vista land grant. The architecture is mainly Spanish Californian in style.

BUENA, 54 *m.,* is a small community center for the surrounding grape-growing country.

SAN MARCOS, 57.3 *m.* (570 alt., 100 pop.), is at the confluence of the Twin Oaks, the Richland, and the San Marcos Valleys (*service station and restaurant accommodations*). This area was originally the *Rancho Los Vallecitos de San Marcos* (Sp., *the little valleys of St. Mark*), a land grant of the Mexican rule. Irrigation water from Lake Henshaw in Warner Valley has augmented the farm and ranch production of this district.

At 57.7 *m.* (L) is a mulberry grove and silk factory (*private*). This corporation-owned enterprise, begun in the late 1920's, is attempting to establish silkworm culture in southern California. It is said that this is the only venture of its kind in the United States.

At 58 *m*, on the floor of the Escondido Valley, are the large packing sheds (R) of a citrus association. Modern machinery has reduced the number of employees to a minimum.

ESCONDIDO (Sp., *hidden*), 63.8 *m.* (650 alt., 3,400 pop.), is the largest inland city in San Diego County. Formerly a part of an old Mexican land grant, the *Rincón del Diablo* (Sp., *devil's corner, or lurking place*), it became the 13,000-acre Wolfskill Ranch in pioneer days. Escondido holds an annual Grape Day Festival on September 9, the town's outstanding event. Harold Bell Wright, the novelist, lives here.

From the junction of Broadway with Grand Ave. (see *Tour* 7A) in Escondido the route goes R. on Grand Ave.

At 64.1 *m.* is a junction with San Diego Ave.; L. on San Diego Ave.

At 66 *m.* is the junction with a dirt road.

> Right on this road to FELICITA PARK, 0.8 *m.*, a natural wooded spot set aside by the county for public recreation. It has picnic grounds, an open-air dance hall, and camping facilities.

At 69.2 *m.* the upper portion of LAKE HODGES is crossed. Boats are rented for fishing and rowing (25c *per hr.*), and bass, trout, crappie, and perch may be caught during the fishing season, May 1 to October 31.

BIG STONE, 78.1 *m.*, a general store, picnic grounds (*adm.* 25c *per car*), and filling station, was named for the many boulders in its vicinity. This region, POWAY VALLEY, was inhabited by Indians in the prehistoric era, and for 50 miles around pictographs (rock pictures) are to be found. From this point southwestward there is a good view of rugged, mountainous terrain.

At 82.1 *m.* is the CREST of POWAY GRADE (952 alt.), a tortuous grade over chaparral covered slopes. Because of limited visibility on curves, the motorist should drive slowly. From the head of the grade westward, the road goes through a portion of the largest privately owned eucalyptus grove in California, a part of the Scripps country estate, Miramar (Sp., *sea view*), whose buildings are to the R.

MIRAMAR, 86.1 *m.*, is a service station on KEARNY MESA, a large, flat tableland.

At 86.8 *m.* is a junction with a paved road.

> Right on this road through CAMP KEARNY, now abandoned, used as a training quarters for recruits during the World War, to a junction with US 101, 11.3 *m.*

LA MISION DE SAN DIEGO DE ALCALA (Sp., *the mission of St. James of Alcala*), 94.4 *m.*, popularly called San Diego Mission (*adm.* 25c) stands on a knoll which rises from the floor of Mission Valley, 6 miles inland.

On July 16, 1769, Fr. Junípero Serra built a crude shelter on Presidio Hill (see *Tour* 1), which became the first in a chain of 21 Franciscan missions in California. Five years later it was moved to its present site, near an Indian village called Nipaguay. The first building was a frame church roofed with tile. In an attack in the early morning of Nov. 5, 1775, Indians succeeded in destroying the church building and in massacring Father Jayme and several others (see *Historical: The Spanish*). In 1780 the new church was dedicated, and from that date the mission prospered. San Diego was the first of the missions to register one

SAN DIEGO MISSION AS IT APPEARS TODAY
(Chamber of Commerce photograph)

thousand baptisms.

In 1803 an earthquake destroyed the buildings, but by 1813 they had been restored, enlarged, and many others added. In 1830-31 the mission owned 8,822 head of cattle, 1,172 head of horses and mules, 16,661 sheep, and had control over 1,506 Indians. Following secularization in 1834, the mission rapidly declined. Richard Henry Dana, in *Two Years Before the Mast,* described his visit there in 1835 as follows: "We drove into the open square in which the stillness of death reigned . . . There was something decidedly striking in its appearance: a number of irregular buildings, connected with one another, and disposed in the form of a hollow square, with a church at one end . . . with . . . five belfries, in each of which hung a large bell, and with an immense rusty iron cross at the top."

The present restoration was accomplished in 1931. Cracks and portions of exposed adobe bricks have been purposely fashioned to create an architectural illusion of the days of the past. Most conspicuous in the design is the symmetrical arrangement of the campanile which rises in three stages and sweeps skyward to the simple wooden cross at its peak. This tower adds grace to the otherwise massive two-storied facade, the central entrance of which is now closed. A gateway to the left of the campanile gives access to the patio, simply landscaped with trees and flower beds. Three small brick crosses commemorate the 450 Indians buried here. The royal arms of the King of Spain may still be seen on a bell in the tower, attesting to its donation in 1802 by the Spanish monarch. The chapel, with a nave 150 ft. long, has no transepts and its plastered walls, 5.5 feet thick, stand 29 feet high. Six long narrow windows high up on the wall give a cathedral lighting to the bare sides, devoid of even the most simple ornamentation. The ceiling is supported by heavy, hewn cross-beams running horizontally from wall to wall, a disappointing feature to those who look for the lofty peaked ceiling of the Gothic and Romanesque-Renaissance architecture. Original paintings, brought to the mission from Spain and bearing the scorched marks of fire from the time of the massacre (*see Historical: The Spanish*) hang near the altar.

Behind the chapel is a room which houses a museum of early relics. Numerous cases are filled with vestments worn by the old padres. Among the books written during the first days of the mission is one containing the signature of Father Junípero Serra, written by the courgeous hand of the man who led early California civilization.

The mission is in charge of the parish of San Diego, and the Sisters of Nazareth conduct a school in the neighboring buildings. In the mission grounds is a reproduction of the Grotto of Lourdes. There are several old olive trees and a cactus hedge, both dating from very early days.

At 94.7 *m.* is SAN DIEGO RIVER, which remains almost dry the greater part of the year. Occasionally, in heavy rain years, it floods the whole floor of Mission Valley.

At 97 *m.* is a junction with El Cajon Blvd. (US 80) ; R. on El Cajon Blvd. to Park Blvd.; L. on Park Blvd. (12th Ave.) to Broadway; R. on Broadway to the central business district of San Diego, 103.2 *m.*

SIDE TOUR 7A

PALOMAR OBSERVATORY

Jct. Mission Rd. and US 395—Pala—Rincón—Palomar Observatory—Valley Center—Escondido.
US 395, Highway to the Stars, Valley Center Rd.
Jct. Mission Rd. to Escondido, 78.2 *m.*
Oiled and paved roads throughout; mountain slopes climbed in wide, easy turns.

Following the San Luis Rey River, this route goes E. through the narrow river valley and ascends Mount Palomar. Returning to the foot of the mountain, it leaves the riverbottom, crosses a low range and enters Escondido Valley.

From the junction of Mission Rd. with US 395, 0 *m.*, the route goes N. on US 395.

At 4.3 *m.* SAN LUIS REY (Sp., *St. Louis, king*) RIVER is spanned by a concrete bridge.

BONSALL, 2.5 *m.*, is a post office, service station, and general store at the converging point of MOOSA VALLEY and GOPHER CANYON, dairy and farming areas. This center was named for a family which settled here in 1874. Moosa is a contraction of Pamoosa (Ind., *happy hunting ground*).

At 3 *m.* is a junction with an oiled road; the route goes R.

Left on US 395 is FALLBROOK, 7.5 *m.* (730 alt., 1,081 pop.).

This area was settled in the 1880's because of its soil and climatic advantages, which make it a good citrus region. In later years avocado orchards were planted and poultry farms established.

At 5.5 *m.* is a junction with a dirt road.

Left on this road to LIVE OAK PARK, 4 *m.,* a natural wooded area set aside by the county for public recreation. It has picnic grounds, an open-air dance hall, and a playground for children.

SAN LUIS REY RANCHO, 9.5 *m.,* is a part of the old Monserate Rancho, granted in 1846 to Ysidro M. Alvarado by Governor Pío Pico. The grant extended S. and E. of the present Fallbrook (see above). The rancho is equipped with race tracks, training tracks, and stables where thoroughbred race horses are bred and trained. Wooden fences enclose riverbottom pasture lands, surrounded by steep canyon walls.

PALA, 14.5 *m.* (444 alt.), site of the PALA INDIAN RESERVA-TION, is the location of LA ASISTENCIA DE SAN ANTONIO DE PALA (Sp., *the chapel of St. Anthony of Pala*), which was built in 1816 by Fr. Antonio Peyri as a branch of the Mission San Luis Rey (see *Tour* 7). Prior to its elevation to the rank of chapel, Pala was one of the many ranchos of Mission San Luis Rey, being first mentioned in a mission report of Dec. 31, 1810. In a short time more than one thousand Indians were converted, which proved the wisdom of the padres in not insisting that all Indians travel to San Luis Rey. Pala was one of the most fertile possessions of the mission.

The story of Pala is the story of the golden age of the California missions, and it is no less the story of the destruction of the mission system. Repeated political disturbances, war, revolutions, and changing regimes left the chapel and storehouses in ruins in less than two decades after the mission was founded. Soon after, the Indians had gambled away their land allotments and were reduced to beggary; in the so-called "squatter period" of American rule they lost or were robbed of their choicest lands, and by 1860 Pala was reduced to absolute ruin.

Following the flood of 1916, Fr. George Doyle launched a movement to restore Pala. Under his direction the *asistencia* was rebuilt, conforming as nearly as possible to the plan of the original structure. It now consists of a *tienda* (Sp., *store*), storerooms, priests' quarters, chapel, and cemetery. An exceptional feature of Pala is the detached campanile, or bell tower, copied from that of the church in Juarez, Mexico. Another interesting feature of the chapel is the mural designs, executed by native workmen and showing in full barbarity the primitive love of color. The floor of the chapel is paved with the original *ladrillos* (Sp., *bricks*).

Pala today is a village of portable frame houses, occupied by Indians. Each of the 176 allottees is given two acres of irrigable land and six acres of dry-farming land. Pala is a subagency of the Mission Indian Agency, which has jurisdiction over Pauma, Rincón, Potrero, and Los Coyotes Reservations.

Annually all Indian tribes in the vicinity meet at Pala Reservation to celebrate the Corpus Christi (Lat., *body of Christ*) Fiesta and the San Antonio (Sp., *St. Anthony*) Fiesta. Corpus Christi is climaxed on Sunday with a high mass and a special sermon. Following the ceremony, a colorful procession parades through the streets to the accompaniment of singing and the pealing of the old mission bells. The similar San Antonio Fiesta, one week later, honors the patron saint of the region.

A *fiesta,* which usually features a rodeo, is held annually on August 25th. Tribal customs, rituals, and legends are fast being forgotten; American swing music, crap shooting, and card playing have all but replaced the Indian chants, dances, and primitive games. Many of the Indians are well educated and have invested a little money wisely; many drive automobiles.

> Left from Pala to a MINE, 1 *m.,* where the rare gem, kunzite, was discovered. The only other place the stone has been found is on the island of Madagascar.

From RINCON (Sp., *corner*) STORE, 24.4 *m.,* an Indian trading post and service station, the route continues L.

At 29.7 *m.* is a junction with a paved road; L. here on the Highway to the Stars.

CRESTLINE, 36.6 *m.,* is a campground.

> Left from Crestline, on a dirt road to PALOMAR STATE PARK, 3.2 *m.* Public campgrounds (*free*) have been set aside by the Forest Service (*no other accommodations*).

North of Crestline the highway climbs the precipitous slopes of PALOMAR MT. (6,126 alt.) and follows along the crest, traversing a gently rolling plateau, heavily wooded with pine and white oak trees. Range upon range of brush-covered mountains extends eastward and westward, and those on the far horizon seem turquoise. Deep gorges and steep brushy slopes drop off from the road as it winds its way around the mountain sides.

PALOMAR OBSERVATORY, 41.4 *m.* (5,568 alt.), was erected for the California Institute of Technology and the Carnegie Institution of Washington, with funds appropriated by the Rockefeller Foundation. After a 5-year study of suitable locations, the 720-acre site on Palomar Mt. was chosen. It is located far from any probable urban development and is therefore free from the night lights that hinder astronomical work. This general location was studied by Professor Hussey more than 30 years ago and discussed in his survey report to the Carnegie Institution. His report was the basis for the selection of the Mount Wilson Observatory site, near Los Angeles. Professor Hussey was favorably impressed with Palomar Mt., but he considered that it was too isolated to be satisfactory for use at that time.

The buildings and equipment include the observatory structure for the 200-inch mirror, cottages for astronomers and scientists, a 1,000,-000-gallon water reservoir, a 50,000-gallon water tank, a 25,000-gallon oil storage tank, an observatory for the 18-inch Schmidt telescope, a dormitory for the staff of workers, and electrically operated pumps drawing 17,000 gallons of water daily from springs on the site.

The main observatory rises 128 ft. and has a dome 135 ft. in diameter. The tube of the telescope is to be about 20 ft. in diameter and 60 ft. long, and will weigh about 125 tons. This includes the 200-inch mirror, lying on a special support system at the lower end of the tube. The glass disc weighs about 16 tons.

The telescope tube is rigid, carrying observers in the cartridge-shaped

110

ARCHITECT'S DRAWING OF THE 200-INCH TELESCOPE
BEING CONSTRUCTED ON MT. PALOMAR

room at its upper end. It turns freely to all parts of the sky and auto-
matically, with great precision, follows the apparent E. to W. motion of
the stars. The total weight of the moving parts of the telescope, including gears and accessories, is about 425 tons.

Other optical instruments used in conjunction with the telescope
enable the observer to photograph celestial objects and to study them with
spectroscopes, photoelectric cells, and special auxiliary apparatus at several
different points. The reflecting mirror has great light concentrating
power, enabling it to reflect very remote celestial objects. After completion of the project, the mirror, its mounting, and the controlling machinery may be viewed through special glass windows from the visitors
gallery.

Return to Rincón Store, 58.4 *m.*, by the same route; L. here on the
Valley Center Rd.

South of Rincón are the rock-strewn wastes of BEAR VALLEY and
HELLHOLE.

At 60.1 *m.* SAN LUIS REY RIVER, which rises in Warner Valley
(see *Tour 8A*), is crossed.

At 60.2 *m.* the route enters the RINCON INDIAN RESERVA-

111

TION (800 alt., 170 pop.). On August 24th, annually, Indians from surrounding reservations meet at Rincón for a 3-day fiesta.

At 63.8 *m.* is a junction with a dirt road.

> Left on this road to SAN PASQUAL INDIAN RESERVATION, 3 m. Eight adult Indians live in this lonely "Hellhole" district.

VALLEY CENTER, 69.4 *m.* (2,110 alt.), is the trading post for a mountain farming and cattle ranching section.

At 77.9 *m.* is a junction with State 78 in Escondido (see *Tour* 7). R. here on State 78.

> Left on State 78 to the SAN PASQUAL BATTLEFIELD, 6.7 *m.* Here on the morning of Dec. 6, 1846, Brig. Gen. Stephen W. Kearny led an ill-advised charge against the California army under Gen. Andres Pico. This battle was the most notable of the California War. (See *Historical: The Americans.*) The American force retreated with a loss of 19 killed and 17 wounded. The Californians were practically untouched. This site is preserved as a State Park. The bodies of the victims are buried at Bennington Cemetery on Point Loma, San Diego (see *Tour* 2).

At 78.2 *m.* is the junction with US 395 (see *Tour* 7).

TOUR 8

THE BACK COUNTRY

San Diego—Laguna Mts.—Julian—Ramona—Mission Valley—San Diego.
US 80; State Highway 73 (Sunrise Highway), 78, and 79; Mussey Grade Rd.; Mission Valley Rd.
San Diego and return, 142.2 *m.*
Usual accommodations on major portion of route; accommodations limited to infrequent campgrounds and service stations E. of Julian. Paved and oiled highway throughout; open all seasons; travel hazardous on oiled mountain grades through Laguna and Julian districts during and following rain and snowstorms.

CAUTION: Use skid chains in Laguna Mts. during snows. Take extra motor fuel, food, water, a tow rope, gunny sacks, and adequate spare tire equipment for any desert trips not designated below.

From sea level at San Diego the route goes E. through an agricultural and horticultural area, rises over mountain grades, and passes through upland valleys to the Laguna Mts. (6,220 alt.), a year round outdoor recreation ground; and then N. over pine-dotted slopes on the western edge of the Colorado Desert to Julian, famous gold-mining district of pioneer days. Returning to San Diego, the route descends SW. through a series of canyons and over rolling, chaparral-covered slopes to the San Diego River, which it follows through the Mission Valley to the coast. A side trip goes E. from Julian (4,219 alt.), to a small, bowl-like valley on the upper reaches of the desert (500 alt.).

At 8.2 *m.* is a junction with College Ave.

> Left on College Ave. to SAN DIEGO STATE COLLEGE, 1.1 *m.* The college buildings, of modified Moorish architecture, are grouped around a quadrangle. Cut from native diorite, *The Aztec,* a brooding black figure sculptured by Donal Hord, sits in one corner of the square (see frontispiece). AZTEC BOWL (L), a football stadium

with a seating capacity of 35,000, is in a natural canyon. East (R) of the college looms BLACK MT. (1,590 alt.), a huge letter S branded on its brushy slopes.

At 9.4 *m.* is a junction with Seventieth St. (Lake Murray Blvd.).

Left on this road to MURRAY DAM AND LAKE, 1 *m.* Following the flood of 1916, water from this reservoir was the only source of supply for the city of San Diego for some time. Motorboat races frequently are held here.

LA MESA (Sp., *the plateau*), 12 *m.* (538 alt., 2,513 pop.), is a residential city. There are many fine homes and country estates in the surrounding foothills. La Mesa's annual fall flower festival attracts county-wide attention. In the 1880's the brush-covered mesa, watered from natural springs on the table-land, was used for grazing sheep. In frontier days, quail and rabbit were so plentiful that a woman who ran a boarding house served wild game daily. Although wild deer also abounded, venison steaks were not regarded highly in those days.

At 13 *m.* is a junction with an oiled highway.

Right on this road to MOUNT HELIX, 1 *m.* (1,380 alt.), topped by a cross 30 ft. high. The name Helix (Lat., *spiral*) was suggested by the winding road leading to the AMPHITHEATER, where impressive sunrise services are held on Easter morning. The summit affords a comprehensive view of San Diego city and bay and of the mountainous back country eastward.

EL CAJON (Sp., *the box*), 16.5 *m.* (450 alt., 1,050 pop.), is the smallest incorporated city in the county. EL CAJON VALLEY is a fertile spot noted for the production of wine and table grapes and citrus and deciduous fruits. The padres of the San Diego Mission once pastured stock in the valley, which was then called Santa Mónica.

FLINN SPRINGS, 24.1 *m.*, a public picnic place and campground, lies E. of a region once covered by the smallest grant in California, the 28.39 acres of *La Cañada de los Coches* (colloq. Sp., *valley of the hogs*).

East of Flinn Springs the road climbs rapidly into an area of small creeks and mountain valleys, through a horticultural, ranching, and agricultural district.

ALPINE, 30.7 *m.* (1,860 alt.), a health resort, is high enough to be free from the coastal fog; the clear, crisp air is said to be a tonic for sufferers from bronchial and lung disorders.

At 32.4 *m.* the route enters CLEVELAND NATIONAL FOREST (see *General Information*).

The WILLOWS, 33.2 *m.*, is a well-known cabin resort.

VIEJAS INDIAN RESERVATION, 34 *m.*, (L) is in a basin which was named *EL VALLE DE LAS VIEJAS* (Sp., *the valley of the old women*) by the Spanish invaders because the Indian men fled to the hills and left the old women and children behind. The Viejas Indians, about 80 in number, have modern homes and farms with power machinery. The valley was used for the breeding and pasturing of race horses before its acquisition by the government, and is one of the few reservation sites in the county which is considered desirable by the tribesmen.

GUATAY (Ind., *large house*), 45 *m.*, a service station and refreshment counter, was named for GUATAY MT. (5,300 alt.) (R), which the Indians thought to resemble a huge wigwam.

113

PINE VALLEY, 46.7 *m.* (4,016 alt.), has service stations, a roadhouse, general store, post office, and hotel. The valley is studded with pine and oak trees. Cabins and horses are for rent throughout the resort area, and there are bridle trails into the surrounding mountains, which are covered with brushy thickets of manzanita, buckthorn, and sage, and with pine and oak trees.

At LAGUNA (Sp., *lake*) JUNCTION, 47.2 *m.* (4,050 alt.), a service station and restaurant, the route goes L. on State 73.

North of Laguna Junction the oiled highway enters the LAGUNA MTS., an area of chaparral thickets, highland meadows, and forests of oak and pine, on the edge of the Colorado Desert (Imperial Valley).

At 56 *m.* is a junction with a dirt road.

> Right on this road to the CUYAPAIPE INDIAN RESERVATION, 1 *m.* The Lagunas were once the retreat of hosts of tribesmen from the advances of white men, but today this reservation, covering an area of over 5,000 acres, has an enrollment of but five Indians, and these do not reside here permanently.

LAGUNA POST OFFICE, 57.2 *m.* (6,220 alt.), is the center for the resort area.

At the FOREST RANGER STATION, 57.6 *m.,* information is available on rules and regulations for visitors to the Cleveland National Forest. Cabins may be leased from the Service, and public campgrounds have been set aside.

North of the Ranger Station, State 73 goes along rock-buttressed slopes on the edge of the desert, affording several miles of views of the wilderness almost a mile below. The desert precipices, crags, and mountain pinnacles spread out to the far horizon like a giant relief map. Their coloring, a burnt amber under the glaring midday sun, fades to rose, mauve, and purple in the late afternoon and dusk.

At 57.9 *m.* is a junction with a dirt road.

> Right on this road to DESERT VIEW, 0.2 *m.,* offering impressive desert scenery from barren cliffs.

At 59.6 *m.* is a junction with a footpath.

> Right on this path to MONUMENT PEAK, 1.5 *m.* (6,321 alt.). CARRIZO (Sp., *reed grass*) CREEK is seen (R), cutting through the sand hills and badlands; beyond, against the base of the CHOCOLATE MTS., is SALTON SEA, in the northern end of Imperial Valley. In the middle distance to the SE. is the irrigable section of the valley. To the S., jutting out of the flat desert, is SIGNAL MT., just across the international boundary line and stretching to the distant rim of Laguna Salada (Sp., *salt lake*), in Mexico. The most conspicuous landmark on the eastern horizon is PICACHO (Sp., *sharp point*) PEAK (1,945 alt.), among the barren ranges flanking the Colorado River, almost directly N. of Yuma, Ariz. On a clear day San Diego city and SAN CLEMENTE ISLAND, 50 miles offshore, also are visible (W).

At 60.4 *m.* an OBSERVATION TOWER (L) has been built around a gnarled pine. Below is the VALLECITO (Sp., *little valley*) VALLEY. Through binoculars, the OLD ADOBE STAGE STATION of the Butterfield Overland Mail Stages at Vallecito (1858-1861) may be seen. Stirred by tales of ghosts, of buried treasure, of deeds of violence and heroism, San Diego County authorities in 1934 began restoration of the

venerable structure, which was fast returning to the soil (see *Tour 8A*).
At 72.8 *m.* is a junction of State 73 with State 79; the route goes R.
on State 79.

> Left (S) on State 79 to CUYAMACA (Ind., *rain above*) STATE
> PARK, 1 *m.* (4,394 alt.), a resort area centering around CUYA-
> MACA LAKE. The lake is part of San Diego's water supply system,
> and in pioneer days it was known as *La Laguna Que Se Seca* (Sp.,
> *the lake which dries up*).
> Accommodations at the resort include hotels, cabins, and camp-
> grounds; hunting, fishing, boating, swimming, and horseback riding
> facilities are available. (*A charge of 50c a night is made for camping
> in the State Park.*)

At 72.9 *m.* is a junction with a county road.

> Left on this road to the 840-acre INAJA (Ind., *my springs*) INDIAN
> RESERVATION, 7 *m.* (33 pop.), and the 80-acre COSMIT RESER-
> VATION, 7.7 *m.* (unpopulated). The natural beauty of these
> reservations is marked. The land is mostly used for grazing.
> PINE HILLS RESORT, 10.8 *m.* (*lodge and cabin accommodations*).
> At 13.3 *m.* is a junction with State 78 and 79 (see below).

At 80.7 *m.* is a junction of State 79 with State 78. The route
continues N. (L) on State 78, 79.

> Right on State 78 is BANNER, 7.1 *m.* (1,800 alt.), at the foot of
> the BANNER Grade, a campground and picnic ground (*adm. 25c
> and 50c*), which was a mining town in pioneer days. From its
> junction with the main highway, this winding road has dropped
> more than 2,000 ft. The region was overrun by gold-mad miners
> when rich ore was discovered in Julian in 1870 (see below). The
> most important mines at Banner were the Redman and the Golden
> Chariot.
> SCISSORS CROSSING, 12.1 *m.*, in the San Felipe Valley, was so
> named because converging roads form the shape of a pair of scissors.
> The Butterfield Trail crosses at this point (see *Tour 8A*). Before
> the coming of the white man, Indian villages were located in the
> region. These were visited in 1782 by Pedro Fages, who camped in
> the valley and gave it its present name.
> BOREGO, (Sp., *borrego, yearling lamb*) STATE PARK, 12.5 *m.*,
> comprises approximately 200,000 acres of varied desert and mountain
> scenery.
> SENTENAC CANYON BRIDGE, 16.7 *m.*, GRAPEVINE MT. is L.
> At 18.3 *m.* is a junction with Borego Valley Road; the route goes L.
> on this oiled road.
> BOREGO POST OFFICE, 26.4 *m.*, a filling station and trading post,
> is in the BOREGO VALLEY (550-1,000 alt.) a bowl-shaped desert
> basin. Irrigation water for the farms and ranches of this productive
> valley is supplied from wells.
> PALM CANYON CAMPGROUND, 34 *m.* The greatest botanical
> curiosities in the Borego State Park are the many specimens of the
> palm tree (*Washingtonia filifera*), the only native palm tree in
> California. Authorities state that this palm tree is "a residual
> remnant of the days of the sabre-toothed tiger, ancestral horse, camel
> and ground sloth, whose fossils have been found here." At one
> time, perhaps 500,000 years ago, this canyon was a palm-lined shore
> of the Gulf of California.
> Eastward is a vast panorama of desert wasteland. Below the valley
> farms is a tumbled waste of copper-hued badlands, shimmering in
> the sunlight. Beyond a range of glistening white sand hills on the
> horizon is the SALTON SEA.
> The first grove of palms is an hour's hike up Palm Canyon from
> the campground. The narrow gorge is unsuited to automobile or
> horseback travel.

JULIAN, 81 *m.* (4,129 alt.), once the center of feverish mining activity, is now a quiet agricultural and horticultural community. The town offers accommodations, and there are campgrounds and cabins for rent in the surrounding pine-wooded resort areas. In January, 1869, placer gold was discovered near Julian. The same year the Bailey brothers and their cousins, the Julian brothers, moved into the region, established home sites, and staked out a townsite, which they named Julian.

In 1870 Billy Gorman, 13 years old, who had arrived in Julian with his family from Texas, found a piece of white rock with yellow flecks in it. He took the quartz to his father, who opened up a mine which was to become known as the George Washington Mine, commemorating the date of the discovery, Washington's Birthday. News of the strike spread, and for a decade Julian was the center of a gold-mining boom, enlivened with bad liquor, gambling, women, and gold digging, and punctuated by quarrels, pistol shootings, and stabbings. Seventy-five men "drank themselves to death" the first year. Mines were opened for miles around. Among the best known were the Stonewall Jackson, the Cuyamaca, and the North Hubbard. A serious effort was made to transfer the county seat from San Diego to Julian. Twenty-mule teams and wagons were brought in and used for hauling ore to San Diego. About 1880, when mining activity was already dying in Julian, the big boom at Tombstone, Ariz., developed, and in the ensuing gold rush most of Julian was loaded on these wagons and taken to Tombstone. Although mining became impracticable in Julian without expensive machinery, recent attempts have revived some hope that again the town may be a rich and industrious mining center. It has been estimated that more than 15 million dollars in gold has been taken from the district.

West of Julian the route descends toward the coast through a series of canyons and over brushy, rolling hills.

At 81.7 *m.* is a junction with a paved road.

> Left on this road to PINE HILLS RESORT, 2.5 *m.* (*lodge and cabin accommodations*). In this area is CAMP MARSTON, a camp for boys under the supervision of the Y.M.C.A. It was named in honor of the donor of the tract, George W. Marston.

WYNOLA, 85.6 *m.*, is a filling station and elementary school. Designated in the 1880's as a post office, the service has long since been discontinued.

SANTA YSABEL, 88.6 *m.* (2,983 alt.), is a trading center, with a hotel, general merchandise store, post office, filling station, and lunch counter. From here the route goes W. on State 78 through a stock-raising and horticultural area.

WITCH CREEK, 91.2 *m.* (2,609 alt.), is a filling station and trading post for a small mountain farming district. This old upland settlement derived its name from an Indian belief that whoever drinks the waters of the nearby creek will become ill and be pursued by bad luck.

RAMONA, 103.6 *m.* (1,440 alt., 450 pop.), in the SANTA MARIA VALLEY, is noted for its poultry farms. An annual Turkey Day Festival is celebrated. This area, an Indian village during the mission regime, later became famous as the *Rancho Santa María de Pamo,*

PINE VALLEY, A SCENE IN SAN DIEGO'S BACK COUNTRY.
LAGUNA MOUNTAINS IN BACKGROUND *(Public Library photograph)*

which was granted to Don Narciso Botello in 1833. The modern town of Ramona was established in 1886.

West of Ramona the route drops more than 1,000 ft. by way of MUSSEY GRADE.

FOSTER, 116.6 *m.,* containing now but a single home, was for many years an active division point for freight and passengers. Business of this line, the San Diego, Cuyamaca and Eastern R.R., dwindled gradually; after the floods of 1916, when it was found that the tracks between Santee and Foster would have to be completely replaced, service was reduced to Lakeside. Remains of the old tracks still may be seen (R).

At 118.6 *m.* is a junction with a dirt road.

> Right on this road to THUM PARK, 1 *m.,* popularly called Cactus Lands Park, exhibiting many varieties of desert flora.

The SAN DIEGO RIVER, 120.3 *m.,* is crossed by a wooden bridge.

LAKESIDE, 120.5 *m.* (410 alt.), was named because of the proximity of LINDO LAKE, which lies in a COUNTY PARK on the eastern edge of town. The town site, platted in 1887, has changed little, and adobe buildings are still in use. Annual round-ups are held at the Lakeside Rodeos (see *General Information: Annual Events*).

At 120.6 *m.* is a junction with an oiled road.

> Left on this road is a junction with an unpaved road 0.4 *m.;* L. to the BARONA INDIAN RESERVATION in the PADRE BARONA VALLEY, 5 *m.,* named for one of the old Franciscan padres. The reservation consists of approximately 5,000 acres, about 100 acres of which are under irrigation. Annually Indians of the county converge on Barona for the *fiestas* (Sp., *festivals*) held on two successive week ends in August. Ritualistic songs, dances, and games of the tribesmen are all but forgotten, and the *fiesta,* once the big event in reservation life, now consists chiefly of visiting, American dances, baseball, and surreptitious gambling.
> EL MONTE PARK, 4.4 *m.,* is a live oak park with picnic and camp

117

accommodations.

EL CAPITAN DAM, 6.7 *m.*, part of the San Diego city water system, is a rock embankment hydraulic fill type dam (38,000,000,000 gals.), completed in 1935. (*No hunting, fishing, boating, nor accommodations at the present time* (1937).)

At 123.6 *m.* is a junction with Mission Valley Road, an oiled highway; the route goes R. on this road.

SANTEE, 123.7 *m.*, has a grocery store, dairy supply store, and filling station which serve the surrounding agricultural district.

> Right from Santee on a dirt road to EDGEMOOR, 0.3 *m.*, the county farm. The farm owns several modern buildings, including a large dairy barn; and many acres of fertile river-valley land. Across the San Diego River (N), in the FANITA HILLS, are several country estates, among them the home of Alan LeMay, writer of western stories.

West of Santee the route goes through MISSION GORGE, a narrow opening into MISSION VALLEY.

THE OLD MISSION DAM, 128.2 *m.* (R), was built by the padres of the San Diego Mission after 1800. Originally about 12 ft. high, 13 ft. thick, and 220 ft. long, this was the first, and most pretentious, attempt at irrigation in Spanish California. An aqueduct of tile on a cobblestone and cement base took the water to the mission.

At 134.3 *m.* is a junction with US 395; L. on US 395 to El Cajon Ave.; R. on El Cajon Ave. to Park Blvd. (Twelfth Ave.); L. on Park Blvd. to Broadway; R. on Broadway to Fourth Ave., 142.2 *m.*

SIDE TOUR 8A

THE DESERT

Laguna Junction—Jacumba—Plaster City—Scissors Crossing—Warner Ranch—Santa Ysabel.

US 80, Butterfield Trail, State 78.

Laguna Junction to Santa Ysabel, 142.3 *m.*

Route roughly paralleled by San Diego & Arizona Eastern R. R. between Jacumba and Plaster City.

Accommodations and service stations at intervals except on Butterfield Trail (54 *m.*).

Paved highway except Butterfield Trail, which follows dry riverbeds in sections and should be avoided during and following heavy rains; route at its best in spring.

CAUTION: The automobile should be in good mechanical condition, with adequate spare tire equipment. Food, extra motor fuel, at least 5 gallons of water, a tow rope, a shovel, and some gunny sacks should be taken. If wheels sink and spin in loose sand, rear tires should be partially deflated, sand shoveled from in front of wheels, and sacks placed beneath to provide traction.

From the rim of Pine Valley, in the mountainous back country, (see *Tour* 8) the route goes SE. to the floor of the Imperial Valley desert. It climbs NW. through a series of arid valleys on the upper reaches of the desert and emerges in a broad mountain basin (3,165 alt.); then swinging

S. runs between shaggy mountains to the adjoining valley of Santa Ysabel.

LAGUNA (Sp., *lake*) JUNCTION, 0 *m.* (4,040 alt.), is a service station and restaurant at the junction with State 73 (see *Tour* 8).

East of Laguna Junction US 80 runs through a rugged, mountainous country strewn with great boulders, over a terrain which gradually becomes more arid.

BUCKMAN SPRINGS, 2.8 *m.* (3,225 alt.), is a service station and bottling works. Its lithia springs, developed commercially in 1876, are said to have medicinal properties (see *Tour* 9).

At LA POSTA (Sp., *post stage*) 8.3 *m.*, a gasoline service station, is a junction with a dirt road.

> Right on this road to LA POSTA INDIAN RESERVATION, 0.8 *m.*, an area of 3,879 acres occupied by only three Indians.

JACUMBA (Ind., *hut by the water*), 25.9 *m.* (2,800 alt., 400 pop.), is a resort and spa within 200 yards of the Mexican border. Patronized chiefly by residents of Imperial Valley, who occupy mountain cabins in the region during the summer months, the town has all accommodations, including an outdoor plunge and tub baths in waters of asserted medicinal value.

East of Jacumba the route crosses a rocky, wind-swept mesa, where it rains so seldom that vegetation is limited to stunted desert weeds and bushes of the hardiest type. Within a few miles the road drops abruptly over the Mountain Springs Grade to the subsea level of the desert.

BOULDER PARK, 34.7 *m.*, the summit of Mountain Springs Grade, affords an excellent view of IMPERIAL VALLEY.

From SHEPARD'S BRIDGE, 42.3 *m.*, at the mouth of the IN-COPAH (Ind., *mountain people*) GORGE, a rocky gap at the southern rim of the Imperial Valley, US 80 gradually descends to the desert.

COYOTE WELLS, 48 *m.*, a service station and refreshment stand, was a watering place for many years for immigrant wagon trains and denizens of the desert. The summit of SIGNAL MOUNTAIN in Mexico (R), used by the Cocopah Indians for signal fires, now serves as a beacon for aviators.

PLASTER CITY, 56.3 *m.*, is the settlement of a cement company which operates a gypsum mine 25 miles N. Cottages for the employees, a service station, and company buildings make up the colony.

At 56.8 *m.* is a junction with a desert road; the route goes L. This road, now called the Butterfield Trail, was first opened by the Spanish explorer, Pedro Fages, in 1782. The peculiar isolation of this section of the old road has been responsible for its preservation. At first it was used by trappers and emigrants from Mexico, and in the pioneer period it was an important road for overland parties from the East. During the gold days it was known as the Southern Emigrant Road. The majority of the settlers using it came with wagon trains from Independence, Mo., by way of Yuma, Ariz. In 1857 the Butterfield Line was authorized by Congress to carry mail from St. Louis to San Francisco. The first stage arrived in California in 1858, and twice a week thereafter until 1861 the long and strenuous trip was made. Stations were from 12 to 25 miles apart, depending upon the condition of the road. The Troy and Concord coaches, drawn by six and eight horses, or mules, were called "swift wagons" by the Indians, who soon learned that raiding them was more foolish than profitable. At times the stages became veritable traveling arsenals. Every passenger was supposed to be armed and was expected to fight if necessary. The eastern part of the route was infested with Comanche Indians, the middle portion by Apaches, the western section by Yuma and Mojave Indians, and all of it with road agents and accidents. With the outbreak of the Civil War, the Butterfield Line went out of existence, but the Southern Emigrant Trail continued to serve the increasing tide of immigrants. It was used by Gen. Stephen W. Kearny and his men in 1846 on their way to the historic battle of San Pasqual (see *Tour* 7A). Its use, however, did not extend much beyond the 1880's. Of the ten stage stations built in San Diego County by Butterfield, only three remain, Vallecito, Warner and Oak Grove (see below).

CARRIZO (Sp., *reed grass*), 74.8 *m.* (*water available*), is a small water hole at the mouth of CARRIZO CREEK, a broad, dry wash in a pass leading out of the open desert into a series of arid valleys surrounded by formidable desert mountains.

A few fragments of timber and a small pile of crumbling clay mark the site of a BUTTERFIELD STAGE STATION at Carrizo. Eighty yards to the W. of the ruins is the GRAVE of an alleged cattle rustler. A headstone over the rock-covered grave bears the laconic legend, "Frank Fox. Killed 1882." Fox, it is said, was buried "with his boots off," after having been slain while bathing in the alkaline waters of Carrizo Creek.

Northwest of Carrizo the trail winds through a series of cactus-studded flats, but continues to follow dry washes wherever possible. Deep ruts, cut by the wheels of heavily laden immigrant wagons and hurrying stage coaches, are reminders that the exact course of the Southern Emigrant Trail is being followed. In places parallel to the road are trails pounded out by mounted guards who accompanied the Butterfield stages to protect the passengers who usually chose this method of transportation only because their haste was too great to go by Panama or around the Horn. Ocotillo, yucca, tuna cactus (prickly pear), thistlesage, cholla cactus, barrel cactus, and mesquite line the roadway; in the higher altitudes century plants, elephant trees, California fan palms, wild plums, incense shrubs, greasewood bushes, desert sage, juniper, chamiso, and sumac add their coloring to the slopes.

At 89 *m.* is a junction with a dirt road.

Left on this road to AGUA CALIENTE HOT SPRINGS, 0.5 *m.* (*water*).

VALLECITO (Sp., *little valley*), 93.0 *m.* (*water*), is a waterlogged saltgrass *cienega* (Sp., *swamp*), surrounded by thickets of tules, desert-willow, mesquite, and cottonwood.

A camp site with water is beside the rebuilt adobe BUTTERFIELD STAGE STATION, restored in 1934 by San Diego County authorities. The name Vallecito is synonymous with tales of strange apparitions, the most persistent one being that of the ghostly stages which drive up in the dead of night to give rest to gold seekers, long overdue in the California Eldorado.

According to the San Diego *Star,* "a terrible tragedy" was enacted on

Nov. 2, 1870, when "two immigrants had an altercation on Monday last at Vallecito, resulting in the death of both of them . . . they were from Texas and had been quarreling all along the route . . . they took two shots apiece, both of the first shots missing and both of the second shots taking effect . . . one in the breast and the other in the abdomen . . . they were brothers-in-law and their families were present at the time of the difficulty." The wives of the two men buried their husbands beneath a mesquite thicket beside the swamp.

Deserted today are the pitiful "ranches" of the few settlers who took up claims under the Homestead Act along this section of the Butterfield Trail, and only occasionally does a prospector with his pack burro or model-T continue to search for the fabulous "low hill of dark rock, thick with yellow metal," from which Pegleg Smith was reported to have picked up chunks of gold as he traveled through this district.

Northwest of Vallecito the trail, which climbs through Box Canyon, has been improved, but it is so narrow that the hubs of an automobile will almost scrape against the rocky walls.

At 110.5 m. is SCISSORS CROSSING in the San Felipe Valley, a junction of the Butterfield Trail with State 78 (see *Tour* 8). Scissors Crossing received its name from the fact that diverging roads at this point assume the shape of open scissors.

North of the crossing the original Butterfield Trail has been obliterated by improved roads. The route, an oiled highway, goes out of the desert through a pass in the upper end of the San Felipe Valley and enters the Warner Valley, a highland basin containing numerous waterlogged *cienegas* (Sp., *marshes*).

At 128.5 m. is the well-preserved WARNER BUTTERFIELD STAGE STATION.

At 129.5 m. is the headquarters of the 44,000-acre WARNER RANCH, now owned by the San Diego Water Co. Waters of the Henshaw Dam (see below) have somewhat lessened the grazing area of this fertile valley, but it is still one of California's foremost cattle ranches. Called *Valle de San José* (Sp., *valley of St. Joseph*) by Spanish padres when they made their first trip into the valley, and once the pivotal center for three Indian peoples, it was used jointly by the Mission San Luis Rey and Mission San Diego. (See *Historical: The Indians.*) In 1844, Juan José Warner, a Connecticut Yankee christened Jonathan Trumbell, received the grant of the entire *Valle de San José*. He had come to California in 1831 with the Jackson Party, and had taken Mexican citizenship papers. The argonauts of 1849, the passengers of the Butterfield stages, and the rising tide of immigrants during the 1860's and 1870's made Warner Ranch a favored stopping place, and it became famous for its hospitality.

After the secularization of the missions the Indians were allowed to drift back to their ancestral lands and shift for themselves. The Cupeños, who lived on Warner Ranch, were allowed to remain in their long-established *rancherias* (Sp., *villages*) by Warner, though he often complained of their depredations and raids upon his stock. His toleration of them was largely a matter of utility. He needed their labor, for which he paid them $3 a month. Warner moved to Los Angeles after Antonio

Garra, a Cupeño chief, led the hill tribes in a general uprising against the whites in 1851. A man of unquestioned bravery, Garra firmly believed that his cause was worthy, and that he would receive the aid of the Mexicans in ridding California of the "invaders." He was captured by the Cahuillas, a tribe in Riverside County which remained loyal to the whites. The Cahuilla Indians took their prisoner to Los Angeles and surrendered him to the authorities. Returned to San Diego, he was tried by court martial and shot.

In 1880 John G. Downey, a former governor of California, owned Warner Ranch, and the Indians' right to occupy the land again became a matter of controversy. A suit was taken to the Supreme Court of California, which decided that the Indians had no right to the land. The government bought 3,438 acres in the Pala Valley, near the Pala Mission Chapel (see *Tour* 8), and in 1903 the Indians were removed forcibly to their new home.

At 130.5 *m.* is the junction with State 79; the tour goes L.

> Right on State 79 to WARNER SPRINGS, 3.6 *m.* (3,165 alt.), a mineral springs resort. Cabins, camping, and hotel facilities are available. Spanish-type buildings in a setting of elm and locust trees cover the site of Agua Caliente (Sp., *hot water*), once a populous Indian village.
> HOT SPRING MOUNTAIN (6,535 alt.) is R.
> OAK GROVE, 14.9 *m.* (well-preserved Butterfield Stage Station).
> AGUANGA, 21 *m.* (Butterfield Station in ruins).
> TEMECULA VALLEY, junction US 395, 38.3 *m.*

MORETTIS, 134.9 *m.*, is the junction with a dirt road.

> Right on this road 4 *m.* to LAKE HENSHAW (hunting, boating, fishing); and 31 *m.* to PALA INDIAN RESERVATION AND MISSION (see *Tour* 7A).

South of Morettis the route leaves Warner Valley and enters the Santa Ysabel Valley through a pass between the MESA GRANDE MOUNTAIN, (R)., and VOLCAN MOUNTAIN, (L). The route skirts the SANTA YSABEL (VOLCAN) INDIAN RESERVATION (L), (9,673 acres, 249 pop.). This reservation has some forest areas of cedar and white oak trees.

At 140.3 *m.* is the junction with a dirt road.

> Right on this road to the MESA GRANDE (Sp., *big plateau*) INDIAN RESERVATION, 7 *m.* (5,963 acres; 227 pop.). This reservation consists mainly of grazing land. It is situated in mountains on which are many oak groves.

SANTA YSABEL CHAPEL, 140.7 *m.*, is a concrete building (L), built in 1924 on the site of an adobe *asistencia* (Sp., *chapel*), which was erected in 1821-22 by the padres of Mission San Diego to serve the Indians of the region.

Santa Ysabel was never as important as the chapel of Pala (see *Tour* 7A). Mexico, after declaring its independence in 1822, began confiscating the mission lands. Though the mission fathers continued a demoralized work until as late as 1846, the *asistencias* were the first to be hard hit. Most of them fell into ruins before the main missions did. After 1850, services at Santa Ysabel were revived, and when the condition of the chapel made it unfit for use, the Indians continued their religious services in the open. Today no Indians live at Santa Ysabel, the communicants of this chapel coming from the Volcan Mountain vicinity, where the Santa Ysabel Reservation is located, and from Mesa Grande Reservation.

At 140.8 *m.* is EL CAMPO SANTO (Sp., *the cemetery*), of the Santa Ysabel Chapel. This burial ground has been used by the Indians since about 1820. Nearby are the *enramadas* (Sp., *arbors*) made of green boughs brought down from the surrounding hills, where the Indians gather twice a year to celebrate traditional festivals. Present-day *fiestas* (Sp., *festivals*) consist chiefly of desultory gossip, baseball games in the afternoon, and American dances, crap shooting, and card playing at night, for the Indian has all but forgotten ancient rituals, dances, and legends.

At 142.3 *m.* is SANTA YSABEL, the end of the tour (see *Tour* 8).

If quick return to San Diego, 43.1 *m.,* is desired, leave route of *Tour* 8 at Santee. Left at Santee to El Cajon; R. on US 80 at the junction of Magnolia Avenue and Main Street.

TOUR 9
CAMPO ROAD

San Diego—Lemon Grove—Dulzura—Campo—Morena Lake—Buckman Springs.
State 94; Buckman Springs Road.
San Diego to Buckman Springs, 60.7 *m.*
Usual accommodations.
Paved road throughout, open all seasons.

This route, which once carried all southern traffic from Imperial Valley, is little traveled. It curves past emerald pastures, shoots down into green, bowl-like valleys, clings to the sides of rocky defiles, and finally wanders through the Campo region, oak-grown park land.

From Fifth Ave. and Broadway in downtown San Diego, 0 *m.,* the route goes E. on Broadway to Thirtieth St., R. on Thirtieth St. to F St., and L. on F St. (State 94).

LEMON GROVE, 8.7 *m.* (460 alt.), is a center for tomatoes and lemons. Shipments are made to all parts of the United States. In the 1880's this area was noted for sheep raising.

The route goes L.

At 10.2 *m.* is the junction with a paved road. The route goes R.

Left on this road to LA MESA, 1 *m.* (See *Tour* 8.)

SPRING VALLEY, 11 *m.* (425 alt.), in early days was an Indian village, and after the American occupation became homestead land. It is a prosperous fruit-raising area. The Spring Valley homestead once belonged to Hubert Howe Bancroft, noted historian. Called by the Indians, *Neti,* the district was named by the Spaniards, *Las Fuentes de San Jorge* (*The Springs of St. George*). The original homestead was made in 1865 by Capt. Rufus Porter, a well known Old Town character. His adobe house (*private*), built in the 1850's, is still occupied. Its timbers are part of the hull of an old coaling vessel, the *Clarissa Andrews,* which went ashore in San Diego harbor near La Playa.

At 13.3 *m.* is the entrance to the CALAVO GARDENS, a recent

123

real estate subdivision, and a center for avocado raising. The orchards stretch back toward MOUNT HELIX, 3 miles NW.

At 14.1 *m.* is a junction with a dirt road.

> Left on this road to SWEETWATER LAKE AND DAM, 8 *m.* (98 ft. high; 9,777,000,000 gallons capacity). Completed in 1888, it was considered one of the great engineering triumphs of its day. The Sweetwater Lake area was a popular picnic ground during the 1890's.

At 14.5 *m.* is a junction with an unpaved road.

> Left on this road lies the HILLSDALE AGRICULTURAL DISTRICT, producing a variety of poultry, livestock, and vegetable products.

SWEETWATER RIVER, 14.9 *m.*, flows into Sweetwater Lake.

At 16.9 *m.* is a junction with an unpaved road.

> Left on this road to JAMACHA, (Sp., corruption of Ind., *Hom-mich-cha, a wild gourd*), 1 *m.* (1,575 alt.). In 1770 an Indian village was in this valley, and it is believed that the raiders who destroyed San Diego Mission in 1775, killing Father Jayme, came from this place. (See *Historical: The Spanish.*) A legend of local interest places the famous lost Pegleg mine 3 miles E. of Jamacha.

INDIAN SPRINGS, 18.9 *m.* (860 alt.), was named in 1919, because of the evidence of an ancient Indian village on this site.

JAMUL (Ind., *slimy water*), 19.2 *m.* (1,040 alt.), in a chain of low-lying foothills, is one of the oldest of the Indian place names which persisted through the Spanish period. The farmers of this area are experimenting with the raising of tobacco, but honey has been the basic product for many years. The mission fathers used this region for wintering livestock. It was converted into a Mexican land grant about 1831, and given to Don Pío Pico. In 1839 an Indian raid occurred here in which, to quote the authorities, "two young maidens were carried off and forced to submit to the vilest outrages."

On SAN MIGUEL PEAK (3,575 alt.), 4 miles distant (R), stands an airplane beacon. Plainly visible from the sea, San Miguel was a landmark to early navigators. Joaquin Miller, California poet, climbed to the summit in 1888, planting some trees there. In the 1890's it was a favorite climb for local residents, and a tourist service offered passage to the top on burros.

> Left from Jamul on Barrett Lake Road to LYONS VALLEY, 10.4 *m.* at which point the route enters the CLEVELAND NATIONAL FOREST (see *General Information*), and to BARRETT LAKE AND DAM, 14.6 *m.* The valley was named for General Lyon, of Civil War fame, who owned a quarter-section of the land. Barrett Lake (171 ft. high; 13,979,000,000 gallons capacity) has a gravity section, arched concrete dam. To facilitate the transportation of building materials, a road was built from Dulzura which had to be hewn from the solid mountain. This region is popular with sportsmen.
> South on this road, which leaves Cleveland National Forest at 15.7 *m.*, to Barrett, 20.6 *m.*, and State 94.

At 23.9 *m.* is the junction with Telegraph Canyon Road.

> Right on this road, passing through TELEGRAPH CANYON, are two of San Diego's important reservoirs. The first telegraph line to San Diego passed through this canyon in 1870. Today the un-

frequented area is a favorite spot for quail and rabbit hunters.

LOWER OTAY LAKE and SAVAGE DAM, 8 *m.* (145 ft. high; 18,353,300,000 gallons capacity). The dam, named for H. N. Savage, former city engineer of San Diego, is a gravity section, arch-type structure. It replaced, the old dam which washed out in the great flood of 1916.

UPPER OTAY LAKE AND DAM, 10 *m.* (86 ft. high; 835,700,000 gallons capacity), is an arch-type, concrete structure. It was built in 1900 and is one of the most highly stressed dams in the world.

COCKATOO GROVE, 13 *m.*, was formerly a stage station on the old Campo Road.

DULZURA (Sp., *sweetness*), 27.3 *m.* (1,100 alt.), is a center for milk and honey production. The name is said to have originated in a curious manner. A hungry wayfarer, who asked a pioneer for food, was answered: "You're mighty welcome, but all I have is milk and honey." The traveler replied: "If I've reached the land of milk and honey, here's where I stay!"

ENGINEER'S SPRING, 28.8 *m.*, is a small spring with a limited supply of water. A party of engineers camped here in the early days of San Diego's efforts to develop a direct railroad route to the east.

BARRETT, 33.2 *m.* (900 alt.), is located in bowl-shaped Cottonwood Valley.

At 38.3 *m.* is the junction with the Tecate Road.

Right on this road is TECATE, 2.6 *m.* (1,900 alt.), situated in a rich agricultural valley which lies mainly in Mexico. There is a splendid U. S. customhouse here and Mexico has a huge stone structure across the line. Grain is raised extensively, Tecate in Mexico having a large flour and malt mill to care for production. Tecate's history dates back to the early 1830's, when Don Juan Bandini obtained this area as a land grant from the Mexican government. In 1837 Indian raids began which harrassed the ranchers for 3 or 4 years. Valentin, an Indian leader of the 1870's, operated in this area and made frequent raids into American territory. Tecate was established in the early 1880's with the opening of a general store by a man named Greer.

POTRERO, 40.3 *m.* (2,323 alt.), is in a well-watered mountain valley, and during the pioneer era was a favorite farming area. After 1890 its population dwindled away, however, and at the present time the principal activity is the raising of race horses.

CANYON CITY, 45.4 *m.*, is a service station, a store, and a few cabins. The only international railroad tunnel in the United States is located S. of this community. The San Diego & Arizona Eastern R. R. leaves Canyon City and crosses into Mexico, returning to United States soil at San Ysidro, across the border from Tijuana.

CAMPO (Sp., *field*), 49.2 *m.* (2,543 alt.), is the business center of CAMPO VALLEY (*good hotel and camping facilities*). In pioneer days this valley was settled by emigrants from Texas, and was known locally as Little Texas or New Texas. A thick-walled, two-storied HEWN-STONE BUILDING, built in 1870, stands on the bank of Campo Creek near the present post office. This was the second building erected in Campo. The first, a store, straddled the creek where the bridge stands; and because ice refrigeration was unknown in that area, the storekeeper preserved milk, butter, eggs, and fruit by submerging them in the cold creek water.

125

Pioneering in this area was beset with many hardships other than the physical work of clearing a wilderness. Outlaws were common in the old West, and in this border region many of them were Mexican. A raid of the late 1860's was perhaps the most famous in Campo history. Six Mexicans came across the line in a heavy covered wagon drawn by six horses. Halting the team a short distance from the general store, they dismounted and with guns ready moved on the store. Seeing the store-keeper standing in the doorway, the bandits opened fire. Wounded, the man fell to the floor, dragged himself to a trapdoor, through which he dropped to the creek bed, and from there returned fire. In this fashion he held them at bay until the shooting attracted the notice of other residents. After the Mexicans had fled, leaving two of their number dead, a posse was formed and captured the remaining four below the international line. On HANGMAN'S TREE, still standing, the gang was given vigilante justice.

The Campo area is noted for hunting and fishing and is well patronized. Duck, quail, and deer may be bagged in season.

At 50.8 *m.* the route goes left on Buckman Springs Road.

Right to junction with U. S. 80 at WHITE STAR, 9.8 *m.*

At 52.2 *m.* is a junction with an unpaved highway.

> Left on this road, which enters the Cleveland National Forest, 1.8 *m.*, to MORENA RESORT, 3.6 *m.*, on MORENA LAKE (*hunting, fishing, camping, and hotel facilities; boats and tackle for hire*).
> At 5.8 *m.* is the MORENA DAM (171 ft. high; 21,900,000,000 gallons capacity). This reservoir is a part of the Otay-Cottonwood water system, belonging to the city of San Diego. It is a rock-fill type dam, which costs less than a concrete structure and is more resistant to earthquakes. In 1915, C. M. Hatfield, a professional rainmaker, well-known in the southwest, used this site for his precipitation plant. Water reserves having been low, because of several dry seasons, the City Council of San Diego entered into a contract with him. Following his efforts, disastrous floods washed out Lower Otay Dam and filled Morena Lake to within 18 inches of capacity. Hatfield tried to collect, and threatened to sue the city. The city fathers retaliated with a threat to sue him for the damage done by the floodwaters of the destroyed Otay Dam. Both suits were dropped.

BUCKMAN SPRINGS, 60.7 *m.* (3,225 alt.), at a junction with US 80, was named for Colonel Amos Buckman, a pioneer of the 1860's, who prospected for gold in this area. The springs are mineral in content and have been developed commercially. The Indians of this vicinity held that these springs were sacred. One of their legends recounts that the lovely Fanita, daughter of Chief Cuyamaca, nursed her lover, Carissa, back to health with the lithia water from the springs.

The route follows US 80 into San Diego, 119.3 *m.*

BIBLIOGRAPHY

Anon. *An Illustrated History of Southern California* (Chicago: Lewis Pub. Co., 1890). 898 pp.

———. *History of San Diego County, California* (W. W. Elliott and Co., 1883). 204 pp.

Adams, H. A. *Story of Water in San Diego* (Chula Vista, Calif.: Denrich Press). 72 pp.

Bancroft, H. H. *History of California* (San Francisco: A. L. Bancroft and Co., 1885). 7 vols.

———. *California Pastoral* (San Francisco: The History Co., 1888). 808 pp.

Bell, Major Horace; Bartlett, Lanier, ed. *On the Old West Coast* (N. Y.: William Morrow, 1930). 336 pp.

Black, S. T. *San Diego County, California* (Chicago: S. J. Clarke Pub. Co., 1913). 2 vols.

Bolton, H. E. *Spanish Exploration in the Southwest: 1542-1706* (N. Y.: Charles Scribner's Sons, 1916). 487 pp.

Burton, Mrs. M. R. *The Squatter and the Don: a Novel of California* (1885). 421 pp.

California. Dept. of Public Works, Division of Water Resources. *San Diego County Investigation* Bul. No. 48, (Sacramento: State Printing Office, 1935). 252 pp. and appendices.

Chapman, Charles E. *A History of California, the Spanish Period* (N. Y.: The Macmillan Co., 1921.) 525 pp.

Chase, J. Smeaton. *California Coast Trails* (Boston: Houghton Mifflin Co., 1913). 326 pp.

———. *California Desert Trails* (Boston: Houghton Mifflin Co., 1919). 379 pp.

Cheney, J. V. *At the Silver Gate* (N. Y.: Frederick A. Stokes, 1911). 99 pp. Poems.

Cleland, R. G. *History of California* (N. Y.: The Macmillan Co., 1922). 502 pp.

Clinch, B. J. *California and Its Missions* (San Francisco: The Whitaker and Ray Co., 1904). 2 vols.

Couts, Cave J.; McPherson, Wm., ed. *From San Diego to the Colorado in* 1849 (Los Angeles: Arthur M. Ellis, 1932). 78 pp.

Culp, Wm. M. *Tumba of Torrey Pines* (San Francisco: Harr Wagner Pub. Co., 1931). 115 pp.

Dana, R. H. *Two Years Before the Mast* (Boston: Houghton Mifflin Co., 1911). 530 pp.

Davidson, Winifred. *Where California Began* (San Diego: The McIntyre Pub. Co., 1929). 170 pp.

Davis, C. C. and Alderson, Wm. A. *The True Story of Ramona* (N. Y.: The Dodge Pub. Co., 1914). 281 pp.

Davis, E. H. *Diegueno Ceremony of the Death Images*, Indian Notes and Monographs, Vol. 7, No. 3, (N. Y. Museum of the American Indian, Heye Foundation, 1919).

Davis, W. H. *Sixty Years in California* (San Francisco: The Leary Co., 1889). 639 pp.

Denis, A. J. *Spanish Alta California* (N. Y.: The Macmillan Co., 1927). 537 pp.

Derby, G. H. (John Phoenix). *Phoenixiana* (Chicago: Caxton Club, 1897). 2 vols.

Dodge, John Mason; Holcomb, William H., ed. *"Jack" (John Mason) Dodge: His Life and His Times* (Los Angeles: Sherman Danby, 1937). 179 pp.

Eldredge, Z. S. *History of California* (N. Y.: The Century Co., ca. 1915). 5 vols.

Ellis, A. J. and Lee, H. E. *Geology and Ground Waters of the Western Part of San Diego County* (Washington: Gov't Printing Office, 1919). 321 pp.

Engelhardt, Fr. Zephyrin. *Mission San Diego* (San Francisco: The James H. Barry Co., 1920). 351 pp.

———. *Mission San Luis Rey* (San Francisco: The James H. Barry Co., 1921). 257 pp.

127

Forbes, Mrs. A. S. C. *California Missions and Landmarks* (8th ed., Los Angeles, 1925). 383 pp.

Garrison, Myrtie. *Romance and History of California Ranchos* (San Francisco: Harr Wagner Co., 1935). 192 pp.

Gilbert, Anna M. *La Mesa, Yesterday and Today* (San Diego: City Printing Co., 1924). 63 pp.

Golden Era Magazine, The.

Goodhue, Bertram G. and Winslow, C. M. *The Architecture and the Gardens of the San Diego Exposition* (San Francisco: Paul Elder and Co., 1916). 154 pp.

Green, F. E. "The Old Mission Dam and Irrigation System" (manuscript). 100 numbered leaves

Guinn, J. M. *History of California* (Los Angeles: Historic Record Co., 1907). 2 vols.

Gunn, Douglas. *Picturesque San Diego* (Chicago: Knight and Leonard Co. 1887). 98 pp.

Hays, J. C. *Pueblo Lands of San Diego* (San Francisco: Mullin, Mahon and Co, 1869). 25 pp.

Heilbron, C. H., ed. *History of San Diego County* (San Diego: San Diego Press Club, 1936). 308 pp.

Herald, The San Diego (newspaper).

Hill, J. J. *History of Warner's Ranch and Its Environs* (Los Angeles, 1927). 221 pp.

Hobby, Carl F. *Sketches of San Diego* (San Diego: Elite Printing Co., 1919). 27 pp.

Hopkins, H. C. *History of San Diego: Its Pueblo Lands and Water* (San Diego: City Printing Co., 1929). 358 pp.

Hunzicker, L. B. and others. "San Diego City and County Place Names" (card index).

Jackson, Helen Hunt. *Ramona* (Boston: Little Brown and Co., 1930). 424 pp.

James, G. W. *Exposition Memories* (Pasadena, Calif.: The Radiant Life Press, 1917). 216 pp.

——. *The Old Franciscan Missions of California* (Boston: Little Brown and Co., 1913). 287 pp.

——. *Picturesque Pala* (Pasadena, Calif.: The Radiant Life Press, 1916). 82 pp.

Johnson, M. E. *Indian Legends of the Cuyamaca Mountains* (San Diego: ca. 1914). 25 pp.

Kelly, Charles. "Reminiscenses" (1900-1924) (manuscript). 42 numbered leaves.

Kettner, Wm.; Steyle, Mary., comp. *Why It Was Done and How* (San Diego: Frye and Smith, 1923). 183 pp.

Kroeber, A. L. *Handbook of the Indians of California*, Bureau of Ethnology, Bul. No. 78 (Washington: Gov't Printing Office, 1925). 995 pp.

Lesley, Lewis B. *The International Boundary Survey from San Diego to the Gila River*, 1849-1850, Quarterly of the California Historical Society, vol. IX, no. 1, (1930).

Marsden, G. *The Field Glass* (Chula Vista, Calif.: The Denrich Press, 1917). 29 pp.

Marston, Mrs. A. L., ed. *Records of a California Family* (1928). 279 pp.

Mayer, P. L. *Historic Landmarks of San Diego* (San Diego: 1930). 26 pp.

McGrew, C. A. *City of San Diego and San Diego County* (N. Y. and Chicago: American Historical Society, 1922). 2 vols.

Miller, Max. *I Cover the Waterfront* (N. Y.: E. P. Dutton and Co., 1932). 204 pp.

Mott, Capt. G. F. *San Diego—Politically Speaking* (San Diego: Frye and Smith, Ltd., 1932). 250 pp.

Municipal Employee, The.

Newcomb, Rexford. *The Old Mission Churches and Historic Houses of California* (Phila.: J. B. Lippincott Co., 1925). 379 pp.

Nolen, John. *San Diego, a Comprehensive Plan for Its Improvement* (Boston: G. H. Ellis Co., 1908). 107 pp.

Orcutt, Eddy and Davidson, Ed. *San Diego, a Brief History*: 1542-1888 (San Diego: Arts and Crafts Press, 1929); jacket title, "The Country of Joyous Aspect." 78 unnumbered pages.

Palou, Fray Francisco; Bolton, H. E., ed. *Historical Memoirs of New California* (Berkeley: The Univ. of Calif. Press, 1926). 4 vols.

Parsons, M. E. *Wild Flowers of California* (San Francisco: Cunningham, Curtiss and Welch, 1914). 417 pp.

Parsons, Theron. "Extracts from His Diaries, 1868-1892" (1925) (manuscript). 100 numbered leaves.

Portola, Gaspar de; Smith, D. E., and Teggart, F. J., eds. *Diary of Gaspar de Portola, During the California Expedition of* 1769-1770, Publication of Pacific Coast History, vol. I (Berkeley: The Univ. of Calif. Press, 1909).

Publications of the San Diego Society of Natural History, Vols. I-VIII (1905-1937).

Rensch, H. E. and E. G. *Historic Spots in California: The Southern Counties* (Stanford Univ. Calif.: The Stanford Univ. Press, 1932). 597 pp.

Requa, Richard S. *Inside Lights on the Building of the San Diego Exposition,* 1935 (San Diego: Frye and Smith, Ltd., 1937). 151 pp.

Richman, I. B. *California Under Spain and Mexico*: 1542-1847 (Boston: Houghton Mifflin Co., 1911). 529 pp.

Rider, A. F. *Rider's California, a Guidebook for Travelers* (N. Y.: The Macmillan Co., 1925). 667 pp.

Robinson, Alfred D. *Life in California* (San Francisco: Doxey Co., 1897). 284 pp.

Rogers, Malcolm. "Stone Art of the San Dieguito Plateau" *American Anthropology* (July 1929).

———. "Yuma Pottery Making" *San Diego Museum Papers,* No. 2 (San Diego: San Diego Museum, 1936).

San Diego. *Port of San Diego* (San Diego: San Diego Harbor Dept., 1937). 66 pp.

San Diego Business (monthly bulletin of Chamber of Commerce).

San Diego Historical Society Files.

San Diego Magazine.

San Diego Yesterdays (San Diego: Book Committee of the D. A. R., 1921). 73 pp.

Saunders, C. F. *The Southern Sierras of California* (Boston: Houghton Mifflin Co., 1923). 363 pp.

———. *Under the Sky in California* (N. Y.: McBride, Nast and Co., 1913). 299 pp.

———. *With the Flowers and Trees in California* (N. Y.: McBride, Nast and Co., 1914). 286 pp.

Smith, W. G. *The Story of San Diego* (San Diego: City Printing Co., 1892). 163 pp.

Smythe, Wm. E. *History of San Diego*: 1542-1908 (San Diego: The History Co., 1908). 736 pp.

Sparkman, P. S. *Culture of the Luiseno Indians,* University of Californa Publications in American Archeology and Ethnology, 8:4 (Berkeley: Univ. of Calif., 1908). 244 pp.

Starkey, M. C. *A Mountain Sanctuary* (San Diego: The Canterbury Co., 1928). 233 pp.

Stewart, George R., Jr. *John Phoenix—the Veritable Squibob* (N. Y.: Henry Holt & Co., 1937).

Strong, Wm. D. *Aboriginal Society of Southern California* (Berkeley: Univ. of Calif. Press, 1929). 358 pp.

Southern Cross, The (official magazine of the Diocese of San Diego).

Southern Jewish Review, The

Sud-California Deutsche Zeitung (German language paper).

Sun, The San Diego (newspaper).

Todd, C. B. *The Battle of San Pasqual* (Pomona, Calif.: Progress Pub. Co., 1925). 23 pp.

Union, The San Diego (newspaper).

Van de Veer, Judy. *The River Pasture* (N. Y.: Longmans, Green and Co., 1936). 213 pp.

Van Dyke, T. S. *Millionaires of a Day* (N. Y.: Fords, Howard and Hulbert. 1890). 208 pp.

———. *The City and County of San Diego* (San Diego: Leberthon and Taylor, 1888). 218 pp.

Walsh, M. T. *The Mission Bells of California* (San Francisco: Harr Wagner Pub. Co., 1934). 327 pp.

Williams, F. S. *Gems of the Southwest* (San Diego: San Diego Printing Co., 1931). Poems.

Wood, Catherine M. *Palomar: from Tepee to Telescope* (San Diego: Frye and Smith, Ltd., 1937). 149 pp.

Wood, N. T. "Daily Journal of Nahum Trask Wood for the Year 1871" (manuscript).

Wright, A. H., comp. and ed. *San Diego and Vicinity* (San Diego: San Diego Herald Press, 1907). Poems.

Zoonooz Monthly.

Map. *California Land,* 1857 (Fitch's Map of San Diego).

First The Blade. An Anthology (San Diego: Neyenesch Printers, Inc., 1933). Vol. 6, 79 pp.

INDEX

Accommodations, 3, 4
Adobe Chapel, 76, 77
Agriculture, 17-18, 45, 52
Agua Caliente, in Mexico, 100
Agua Caliente, Indian village, 122
Agua Caliente Hot Springs, 120
Aguanga, 122
Aguirre, Jose Antonio, 38, 77
Airports, 1, 90
Albright, Harrison, 86
Alcazar Garden, 84
Alexander (ship), 28
Allen, Frank P., 83
Alpine, 113
Altimirano, Jose, 76
Altitude, 9
Alvarado, Juan Bautista, Gov., 32
Alvarado, Ysidro M., 109
American Conquest, 30-36
American Legion Headquarters, 88
Ames, John Judson, 38, 40
Amphion Club, 58
Annual Events, 7-8
Archbold, Richard, 70
Ard-1, U. S. S., 99
Area, 37, 66
Arguello, Santiago, 28
Army Air Corps Hangar, U. S., 90
Artists, 60
Aviation: first hydroplane flight, 44; construction of Spirit of St. Louis, 44; first airmail service, 68; sustained flight record, 69; first circumnavigation of the world, 69; first dirigible transcontinental flight, 69; transcontinental speed record, 69; first regular airmail service, 69; mass flight, 69; first refueling by night, 69; glider record, 69; first transcontinental non-stop seaplane flight, 70
Aztec Bowl, 112
Aztec, The, statue by Donal Hord, 60, 112

Balboa Park: as a city section, 13-15; architecture, landscaping and exhibits, 83-90; miscellaneous reference, 9
Ballast Point, 82
Bancroft, H. H., 123
Bandini, Juan, 31, 32, 36, 75, 77, 125
Bandini, Casa de, 62, 75
Banner, 115
Barona Indian Reservation, 117
Barrett, 125
Barrett Lake and Dam, 48, 125
Battle of San Diego, the, 28
Bay, San Diego, *see* Harbor, San Diego
Bean, Joshua, Mayor, 38

Bear Flag Revolt, 34
Bear Valley, 111
Belgian King (ship), 67
Bennington Cemetery, 80
Bennington disaster, 80
Betsy (ship), 28
Big Stone, 106
Birds, 18-19
Bishop's School, 96
Black Mountain, 113
Bonsall, 108
Booms, 41, 42, 49
Booth, Evangeline, 68
Borego Post Office, 115
Borego State Park, 115
Botello, Don Narciso, 117
Bouchard, Hippolyte, 28
Boulder Park, 119
Boundaries, early county, 37-38
Bowlus, W. H., 69
Boy Scouts, Headquarters of, 89
Box Canyon, 121
Braun, Maurice, 60
Bridge of Long Life, 88
Bridges, Appleton S., Mr. and Mrs., 88
Broadway pier, 1, 94
Broell, P. C., 72
Brown, John, 77
Brown, Royal A., 58
Bryan, William Jennings, 67
Buckman, Col., Amos, 126
Buckman Springs, 119, 126
Buddy, Right Reverend Bishop, 70
Buena, 105
Buena Vista Land Grant, 105
Building Trades Council, 53
Bulletin, Weekly, 46
Bus lines and stations, 1
Butterfield Stage Stations, 119-121
Butterfield Trail, 40, 114, 119-121

Cabrillo, Juan Rodriguez, 14, 24, 82
Cabrillo Anniversary Celebration, 67
Cabrillo Bridge, 83
Cabrillo National Monument, 80
Cactus Garden, 86
Cadman, Charles Wakefield, 58
Cafe of the World, 88
Cahuenga Pass, 33-34
Calavo Gardens, 123
California Building, 84
California National Guard, armory of, 86
California Pacific International Exposition, 69
Californians, the, 29, 54, 56
Camp Kearny, 106
Camp Marston, 116

Campo, 125-126
Cannery Inspection Division, California
    Department of Public Health, 93
Canyon City, 125
Capron Stage Line, 40
Cardiff, 103
Carlsbad, 103
Carrillo, Jose Antonio, 31
Carrillo, Casa de, 74-75
Carrillo, Josefa, elopement of, 54
Carrizo Creek, 114, 120
Carrizo Stage Station, 120
Carson, Kit, 34
Casa del Rey Moro, 87
Cassidy and Vierra, murals by, 84
Catholic Church, 55; *see also* Missions
Cattle industry, 30, 45, 54
Census, 37, 50, 68
Chain stores, 52
Chamber of Commerce, 46, 65
Charters, city, 39, 65, 66, 69
Chinatown, 10, 12, 57
Chula Vista, 100
Church of the Immaculate Conception,
    76, 77
Churches, 40, 62, 66, 76, 77, *see also*
    Missions
City stadium, 67, 90
Civic Center, 12, 70, 93
Civic laxity, early, 39
Clarissa Andrews (ship), 123
Cleveland National Forest, 20, 113, 124
Clubs and societies, 58-62
Coast Guard Station, U. S., 92
Cobblestone Jail, 39, 76-77
Coburn, Walt, 96
Cockatoo Grove, 125
Congress Hall, 75
Consolidated Aircraft Corporation, 45,
    90
Convict soldiers, Mexican, 32
Coronado, 82, 102
Coronado Beach Company, 42
Coronado Ferry slips, 94, 102
Coronado Islands, 102
Corpus Christi Fiesta, 109
Cortes, Hernan, 24
Cosoy (floating bathhouse), 66
Cosmit Indian Reservation, 115
Cosmopolitan Hotel (*Bandini, Casa
    de*), 75
Cota, Casa de, 78
County, *see* San Diego County
County Fair, 103
County Fairgrounds and Racetrack, 103
County Hospital, 67
Courthouse, 66
Couts, Cave J. Sr., 105
Couts, Cave J. Jr., 105
Couts vs. Morales, 39
Coyote Wells, 119
Creole Palace, 57
Crespi, Fr. Juan, 21, 26

Crestline, 110
Crofts, William H., 90
Crosby, Bing, 103
Crosthwaite, Philip, 39
Cupeno Indians, 21, 121-122
Curtiss, Glenn H., 67
Custom House, U. S., 90, 100
Customs, early California, 54-55
Cuyamaca Lake and Dam, 48, 115
Cuyamaca (mine), 116
Cuyamaca State Park, 115
Cuyapaipe Indian Reservation, 114
Cyane (ship), 34

Dams, 45, 48, 67, 68, 69, 124, 125, 126
Dana, Richard Henry Jr., 30, 45, 78,
    107
Davis, William Heath, 38
Dead Men's Point, 94
del Coronado, Hotel, 42, 102
Del Mar, 103
Del Mar Turf Club, 103
Dempsey, Jack, 101
de Furucker, Dr. G., 80
Derby, George H. Lt., 39, 40, 74, 77
Derby dike, 17, 74, 77
Derby House, 77
Descanso, 101
Desert View, 114
Destroyer Base, U. S., 99
Diocese of San Diego, 70
Discovery of San Diego, 24
Discovery, Vancouver's ship, 28
Discovery, the whaler, 29
Doolittle, J. H., Lt., 68-69
Downey, John G., Gov., 122
Downtown San Diego, 12
Doyle, Fr. George, 109
Drama, 60
Duhaut-Cilly, Auguste, 31
Dulzura, 125
Dupont, Samuel F., Comdr., 34, 72

Earthquake of 1803, 107
East San Diego, 15
Echeandia, Jose Maria, Gov., 30-32
Edgemoor, 118
Edison, Thomas, 68
Edward, Prince of Wales, 68
Einstein, Dr. Albert, 69
El Cajon, 113
El Cajon Valley, 17, 113
El Camino Real, 74
El Campo Santo, at Old Town, 76
El Campo Santo, at Santa Ysabel, 123
El Capitan (cannon), 75
El Capitan Lake and Dam, 48, 118
El Cid Campeador, statue by Anna
    Hyatt Huntington, 86
El Cortez hotel, 9
El Jupiter (cannon), 72, 75, 76
El Monte Park, 117
El Portal, 84

Encanto, 15
Encinitas, 103
Encinitas Flower Show (National Mid-winter Flower Show), 103
Engineer's Spring, 125
Ensenada, 101
Episcopalian meeting, first, 65
Escondido, 106
Estudillo, Jose Antonio, 75
Estudillo, Casa de, 75-76
Exploration, early California, 24-26

Factories, 49-50
Fages, Pedro, Gov., 21, 115, 119
Fairbanks, Douglas, Sr., 103
Fairgrounds, San Diego County, 103
Fallbrook, 108
False Bay (Mission Bay), 95
Fanita Hills, 118
Fauna, 18-19
Federal Building (Balboa Park), 86
Federal Music Project, 58
Federal Theater Project, 60
Felicita Park, 106
Ferrell, W. C., 38
Ferrelo, Bartolome, 24
Fiestas, 55, 112, 117, 123, *see also* Corpus Christi Fiesta, San Antonio Fiesta
Figueroa, Jose, Gov., 32
Fine Arts Gallery, 60, 87-88
Fire Department, first organized, 65
Fire of 1872, 72
Fish and Game Laws, 2-3
Fisherman's wharf, 94
Fishing: salt water, 5, 19, 63, 94; fresh water, 5, 63
Fishing industries, 45, 50, 56, 57
Fitch, Henry Delano, 54
Flag raising, marker commemorating first, 75
Flinn Springs, 113
Flood of 1916, 68
Flora: of city, 13, 18; of county, 18, 103, 120
Flower and bulb Industry, 103, 104
Flume, old wooden, 48
Font, Fr. Pedro, 21
Ford, Henry, 68, 86
Ford Bowl, 58, 86
Ford Building, 86
Forest Ranger Station, U. S., 114
Forster, Don Juan, 99-100
Fort Guijarros, 28, 82
Fort Rosecrans, 14, 80
Fort Stockton, 36, 72, 82
Fossils, 19-20
Foster, 117
Fox, Frank, grave of, 120
Fox Theater, new, 69
Franciscan Chapel, 84
"Free Speech" fight, 67
Fremont, John C., Gen., 34, 36

Fries, Herman, artist, 60

Gallant (ship), 64
Galvez, Jose de, 26
Garra, Antonio, 39, 122
Garra Uprising, 39, 122
Gasparra, Father, character in *Ramona,* 77
Gems, 20
Geology of county, 18, 19
George Washington (mine), 116
Getz, Thomas, "Tommy", 76
Giddings and Woods Pack Train, 40
Girl Reserves, 57
Godey, Alexis, 34
Gold mining, 116
Golden Chariot (mine), 115
Golden Hill, 9-10, 16
Goldman, Emma, 67
Goodhue, Bertram G., 62, 83, 84
Gopher Canyon, 108
Grace Lutheran Church, 62
Grape Day, 7, 106
Grapevine Mountain, 115
Gray, Andrew, Lt., 38
Grotto of Lourdes, reproduction of, 108
Grunnion fishing, 19
Guadalupe, 101
Guadalupe Hidalgo, treaty of, 36
Guatay, 113
Gunn, Douglas, 66

Half Way House, 101
Hall of Anthropology, 84
Hammill, Samuel W., 87
Hangman's Tree, 126
Haraszthy, Agostin, 39, 77
Haraszthy, Charles, 39
Harbor, San Diego, 17, 25, 26, 27, 68, 99
Harbor Department Building, 94
Harbor development, 56, 67
Hatfield, C. M., 126
Heindel, Max, 104
Hellhole, 112
Henshaw Lake and Dam, 122
Herald, The, 38, 40, 41, 61, 74
Hewitt, Dr. Edgar L., 84
Hide Houses, 30, 45
"Hide Park" (La Plava), 83
Hide Trade, 30-31, 45
Highway mileage, 53
Hijar, Jose, 64
Hijar Colony, 64
Hill, Henry, 37
Hillsdale Agricultural District, 124
"History of Man," Smithsonian Institution exhibit, 84
Hodges Lake and Dam, 48, 106
Homestead, The, 80
Hord, Donal, statues by, 60, 87, 112
Horticultural Building, 88
Horton, Alonzo E., 12, 40, 41, 56, 66

Horton House, 41
Horton Plaza, 12
Horton's Addition, 40, 41, 72
House of Hospitality, 87
House of Pacific Relations, 86
Hunter, Diego, first child of American parentage, 36
Hunter, Jesse D., Capt., 36
Hunter, Thomas B., 83
Huntington, Anna Hyatt, 86

I Cover the Waterfront, by Max Miller, 60, 90
Imperial Beach, 101
Imperial County, 42
Imperial Valley, 49, 119
Inaja Indian Reservation, 115
Income groups, governmental and retired, 52
Incopah Gorge, 119
Indian Springs, 124
Indian, The, sculpture by Arthur Putnam, 74
Indian Village, 89
Indians, 21-24; tribes, 21; physical and mental characteristics, 21; clothing, 21, 22; rancherias, 22; occupational debris, 22; food, 22, 23; religion, customs, and traditions, 23; attack on mission, 26-28; secularization, 30, 32; population in 1847, 37; liquor sale to, 38; Garra uprising, 39, 121-122; reorientation, 54; intermarriage, 54; pictographs, 106; Viejas legend, 113; removal from Warner Ranch, 122; Jamul raid, 124; Fanita legend, 126; Reservations, Rincon, 109, 111-112; Pala, 109, 110; San Pasqual, 112; Viejas, 113; Cuyapaipe, 114; Inaja, 115; Cosmit, 115; Barona, 117; La Posta, 119
Industry, 49-50
Information service, 8
Ingersoll Collection of Bird's Eggs, 89
International Boundary, 100
International Boundary Survey, 65
International Headquarters of the Universal Brotherhood and Theosophical Society, 80
International Longshoremen's and Warehousemen's Union, 53, 94
International railroad tunnel, 125
Italians, the, 56, 57
Itata (ship), 67
I. W. W., 67

Jackson, Helen Hunt, 60, 75, 77, 104
Jacumba, 119
Jail, first county, 39, 76-77
Jamacha, 124
Jamul, 124
Japanese, the, 58
Japanese Pavilion, 88

Jatay, 101
Jayme, Fr. Luis, 26-28, 106, 124
Jessop Collection of Archery, 84
Johnson, Charles, Capt., 77
Julian, 41, 116
Junipero Serra Cross, 74

Kearny, Stephen W., Gen., 34-36, 75, 112, 120
Kearny Mesa, 106
Kearny Trail Marker, 75
Kelley, Oakley, Lt., 69
Kennedy, Frederick, 62
Kettner, William, Congressman, 78
KFSD, 61
KGB, 61
Kimball Brothers, 41
Kunzite mine, 110

La Jolla, 17, 95-96
La Jolla Caves, 96
La Jolla Library, 96
La Jolla Ruff Water Swim, 96
La Jolla Woman's Club, 96
La Laguna de las Flores, 88
La Mesa, 113, 123
La Mision, 101
La Playa, 14, 30, 38, 83
La Posta, 119
La Posta Indian Reservation, 119
Labor Unions, 52-53
Laguna Junction, 114, 119
Laguna Mountains, 112
Laguna Post Office, 114
Lake, Stuart, 60
Lakeside, 117
Lakes (reservoirs), 48, *see also under definitive names*
Land Grants, 33, 99-100, *see also under definitive names*
Lane Field, 94
Law Digest, 2
Lawlessness under American rule, 37-39
Lelia Byrd (ship), 28, 82
LeMay, Alan, 60, 118
Lemon Grove, 123
Liberty Bell, 68
Libraries, 61, 62, 65, 68, 89, 96
Life in California, by Alfred Robinson, 55
Lily Pool, 84
Lindbergh, Charles A., 44, 78, 90
Lindbergh Field, 90
Lindo Lake, 117
Lindo Park, 117
Live Oak Park, 109
Log rafts, 50
Logan Heights, 16, 56, 57
Loma (ship), 65
Loma Portal, 63, 78
Lopez, Casa de, 77
Los Angeles, 31, 32, 34, 50
Los Coches, La Canada de, 113

Los Surenos Art Center, 60, 89
Lower Otay Dam, 48
Lower Otay Lake, 48, 125
Lyons Valley, 124

Machado, Jose Manuel, Corp., 78
Machado, Casa de, 78
Macready, John, 69
Mammals, 18-19
Marcelli, Nino, 58
Marine Band, U. S., 58
Marine Base, U. S., 78
Maritime trade, early, 31
Markham, Edwin, 60
Marshall, Bill, 39
Marston, George W., 72, 74, 116
Mason, James E., 65
Mason, Walt, 60, 96
Masons, 65, 67
Mayan Gallery, 84
Medanos Point, 17, 95
Merriam, Frank F., Gov., 70
Merritt, Ezekiel, Capt., 34
Mesa Grande Indian Reservation, 122
Mesa Grande Mountain, 122
Methodist Church, first, 66
Mexicans, the, 54, 56-57
Mexican cultural survival, 56-57
Mexican Government Fishing Inspection, 94
Mexican National Highway, 99
Mexican rule, 29-34
Micheltorena, Manuel, Gov., 32-33
Middletown, 13, 14
Military Reservation, U. S., 80
Miller, Joaquin, 60, 124
Miller, Max, 60, 90, 96
Mineral resources, 20
Mining: gold, 41, 116; gems, 20, 110
Miramar, 106
Mission Bay, 17, 95
Mission Bay State Park, 70
Mission Beach, 95
Mission Dam, Old, 118
Mission Gorge, 118
Mission Hills, 13, 14-15, 17
Mission Valley, 14, 74, 82, 118
Missions, 26, 28, 29, 32; see also San Diego Mission, San Luis Rey Mission, San Juan Capistrano Mission
Monserate Rancho, 109
Monterey, 26, 28, 30, 31
Monument Peak, 114
Moosa Valley, 108
Morena Lake and Dam, 48, 126
Mormon Battalion, 36
Morrettis, 122
Mount Helix, 113, 123
Mount Palomar, 108, 110
Mount Soledad, 95
Mountain Springs Grade, 119
Municipal piers, 94

Murray Lake and Dam, 113
Museums, see Serra Museum, Natural History Museum, San Diego Museum
Music, 58
Mussey Grade, 117

Natalie (ship), 64
National City, 41, 48, 99
National City and Otay RR., 66
National Forest Regulations, 2-3
National Guard, California, Armory of, 86
National Mid-Winter Flower Show, 103
Natural History Museum, 89
Naval Headquarters, Eleventh District, 94
Naval Hospital, U. S., 89-90
Naval Quarantine and Coaling Station, U. S., 42, 83
Naval Reserves, U. S., headquarters of, 92-93
Naval Training Station, U. S., 78
Naval Wireless Station, U. S., 68
Navy, U. S., payroll and personnel, 50, see also naval establishments under definitive names
Navy Band, U. S., 58
Navy Field, 94
Navy pier, 94
Negroes, the, 16, 57
Neighborhood House, 16, 57
Nelson, Eric, 69
Newspapers, 60-61; see also under definitive names
Nipaguay, 106
Nolen, John, 44
Nolen Plan, 44
North Hubbard (mine), 116
North Island, 17, 68, 82, 102
North Park, 15
North San Diego (Old Town), 41
Noyes, W. H., 40

Oak Grove Stage Station, 122
Observation Tower, (in Laguna Mts.), 114
Ocean Beach, 95
Oceanside, 104
Old Globe Theater, reproduction of, 84
Old Town: as a city section, 14; houses and sites, 72-78; miscelleaneous references, 34, 36, 38
Old Town Plaza, 14, 75
Oriental population, 57-58
Ortega, J. F., Serg., 26
Osuna, Juan Maria, Mayor, 37
Osuna letter, 37
Otay Lakes and Dams, see Lower Otay, Upper Otay, Savage Dam
Otay Water Company, 48
Otter trade, 45

Our Lady of the Rosary, 62
Overland Mail, first, 65

Pacific Beach, 95
Padre Barona Valley, 117
Paintings, 60
Pala, 109-110
Pala Indian Reservation, 109-110
Palace of Education, 86
Palace of Entertainment, 86
Palm Canyon, in Balboa Park, 84
Palm Canyon, in Borego State Park, 115
Palm Canyon Campground, 115
Palm City, 101
Palomar Mt., 108, 110
Palomar Observatory, 108, 110
Palomar State Park, 110
Palou, Fr. Francisco, 21, 22, 26, 72-74
Palou Monument, 72-74
Panama-California Exposition, 42-44, 88
Pantoja Park, 38
Parks and Plazas, see under definitive names
Parry, Dr. C. C., 98, 103
Pattie, James Ohio, 31
Pattie, Sylvester, 31
Pattie's Narrative, by J. O. Pattie, 31
Payroll: fishing, 50; Government, 50; W. P. A., 52
Pedrorena, Miguel de, 36, 37, 38, 76
Pedrorena, Casa de, 76
Pegleg (mine), 124
Pendleton, George, 77
Pendleton House (Derby House), 77
Pepper Tree Grove, 89
Peyri, Fr. Antonio, 104, 109
"Phoenix, John", pseudonym of G. H. Derby, 40
Phoenixiana, by G. H. Derby, 40, 61, 77
Photographic Arts Society, 60
Piccarilli, Furio and Attilio, sculpture by, 84
Pichaco Peak, 114
Pico, Andres, Gen., 34, 36, 112
Pico, Pio, Gov., 31, 33, 123
Pictographs, 106
Piers, 1, 94, 95, 104
Pine Hills Resort, 115, 116
Pine Valley, 114
Plaster City, 119
Plaza de los Estados, 86
Plaza de Panama, 86, 87
Point Guijarros, 28
Point Loma: as a city section, 14; places of interest, 78-83; miscellaneous references, 17, 25, 30, 31, 56
Point Loma High School, 80
Point Loma Lighthouse, 82
Point Lowa Post Office, 14, 83
Population, 29, 42, 49, 70
Porter, Rufus, Capt., 123
Portola, Gaspar de, Gov., 26, 74

Portuguese, the, 14, 56, 57, 83
Post Exchange, 82
Potrero, 125
Poway Grade, 106
Poway Valley, 106
Presidio, the (El Presidio Real), 26, 29, 31, 74
Presidio Hill Park, 72-74
Public buildings, 1-2
Public Library, 61, 62
Public Riding Academy, 90
Public utilities, 53
Putnam, Arthur, bronzes by, 74, 88

Racial minorities, 56-58
Railroads, see under definitive names
Railroad station, 1
Rainfall, 18
Ramona, 116-117
Ramona, by Helen Hunt Jackson, 60, 75-76, 77, 105
Ramona's Marriage Place, 75, 76, 77
Rancho Guajome, 105
Rancho Los Vallecitos de San Marcos, 105
Rancho de la Nacion, 99
Rancho, San Luis Rey, 109
Rancho Santa Fe, 103
Rancho Santa Margarita, 33
Ranchos, see Land Grants and definitive names
Reade, Lt., 66
Recreation, 4-6
Redman (mine), 115
Reiffel, Charles, 60
Reitman, Ben, 67
Reservoirs, see Lakes
Retail stores, 52
Reynolds, John, Rev., 65
Riding Academy, public, 90
Rigel, U. S. S., 99
Rincon del Diablo, 106
Rincon Indian Reservation, 109, 111-112
Rincon Store, 110, 111
Rivera y Moncada, Capt., 26
Rivers, list of principal, 17
Robinson, Alfred, 33, 55
Robinson, Yankee Jim, 39, 76
Rockwell Field, 102
Rogers, Malcolm, 22
Roman Catholic Church, see Catholic Church
Roosevelt, Franklin Delano, Pres., 78
Roosevelt, Theodore, 68, 80
Rosarito Beach, 101
Rose, Louis, 83
Rosecroft Begonia Gardens, 80
Roseville, 14, 83
Rosicrucian Fellowship, 104
Rowan, Stephen C., Lt., 34
Ruiz, Francisco Maria, Capt., 72, 75
Ryan Aeronautical Company, 90

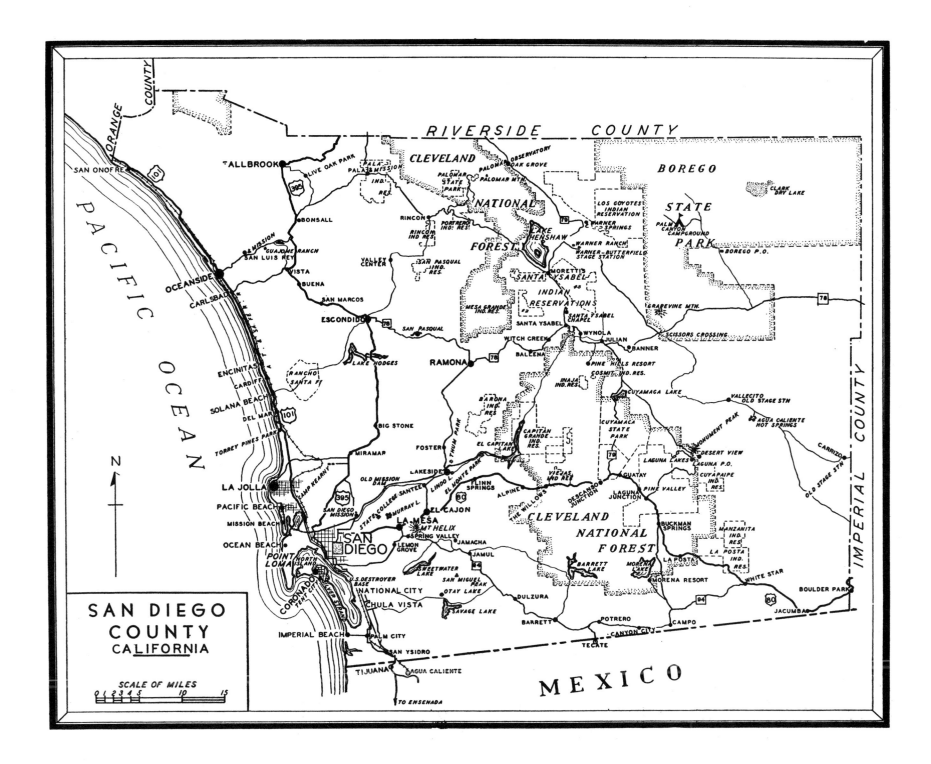

SAN DIEGO
COUNTY
CALIFORNIA

SCALE OF MILES
0 1 2 3 4 5   10   15

Ryan Flying Field, 78
Ryan School of Aeronautics, 1, 90

Sachem (ship), 30
Salton Sea, 114, 115
San Antonio (ship), 26
San Antonio Fiesta, 109
San Antonio de Pala, *see* Pala Chapel
San Carlos (ship), 26
San Diego de Alcala, 25, 88
San Diego de Alcala, *see* San Diego Mission
San Diego and Arizona Eastern RR., 42, 49
San Diego and Cuyamaca Eastern RR., 117
San Diego Fine Arts Society, 60, 88
San Diego Flume Company, 48
San Diego and Gila RR., 40
San Diego Historical Society, 74
San Diego Mission, 26, 28, 29, 106, 118
San Diego Museum, 84
San Diego Open Forum, 61
San Diego Padres, 63, 94
San Diego River, 17, 74, 77, 108, 117
San Diego Rowing Club, 95
San Diego Senior High School, 13, 90
San Diego Society of Natural History, 89
San Diego State College, 61, 112
San Diego Symphony Orchestra, 58, 86
San Diego Water Company, 48
San Dieguito Mutual Water Company, 48
San Felipe Valley, 115, 121
San Jose (ship), 26
San Juan Capistrano Mission, 28
San Luis Rey Mission, 104-105, 109
San Luis Rey Rancho, 109
San Luis Rey River, 103, 105, 108
San Luis Rey Valley, 103, 104
San Marcos, 105
San Marcos Land Grant (*Los Vallecitos de San Marcos*), 105
San Miguel (San Diego), 24
San Miguel Peak, 124
San Pasqual, battle of, 34-36
San Pasqual Battlefield, 75, 112
San Pasqual Indian Reservation, 112
San Salvador (ship), 24
San Ysidro, 100, 101
Santa Fe Railroad, 42, 48, 89
Santa Maria Land Grant (*Rancho Santa Maria de Pamo*), 116
Santa Maria Valley, 116
Santa Ysabel, 28, 116, 123
Santa Ysabel Chapel, 28, 122-123
Santa Ysabel Indian Reservation (Volcan), 122-123
Santee, 118
Santiago, Fr. Juan N. de, 104
Santo Tomas (ship), 25

Savage, H. N., 125
Savage Dam, 125
Savoy Players, 60
Schools, 13, 61, 65
Schroeder, Albert, 62
Schultz, Gustav, 96
Schumann-Heink, Mme. Ernestine, 70
Scientific Library of Natural History Museum, 89
Scientific reference library, founding of, 68
Scissors Crossing, 115, 121
Scott, Tom, 41
Scripps, Ellen B., 88, 89, 96
Scripps, Robert, 89
Scripps Country Estate, 106
Scripps Institution of Oceanography, 96
Scripps Memorial Hospital and Metabolic Clinic, 96
Scripps pier, 98
Sentenac Canyon Bridge, 115
Serra, Fr. Junipero, 26, 72, 74, 106
Serra Cross, 74
Serra Museum, 74
Serra Palm Tree, 74
Sessions, Kate, 15
Shenandoah (dirigible), 69
Shepard's Bridge, 119
Shopping District, 6, 10, 12
Shore Acres, 100
Signal Mountain, 114, 119
Silvas, Maria Antonia Machado de, 78
Silver Strand, 17, 82, 101-102
Sisters of Nazareth, 108
Smith, Albert B., 34
Smith, Jedediah, and party, 31
Smith, Lowell, 69
Smith, Pegleg, 121
Snowstorm of 1882, 66
Snyder Continuation School, 90
Soils, 17, 18
Solana Beach, 103
Solar Aircraft Company, 92
Southern California Mountain Water Company, 48
Southern Cross, The, 60
Southern Emigrant Road (Butterfield Trail), 119, 120
Southwestern Jewish Review, 60
Southwestern Yacht Club, 93
Spalding, A. G., 80
Spanish culture in California, 55
Spanish rule, 26-29, 54
Spanish Lighthouse, Old, 80-82
Spanish Village, 60, 89
Speer Flying Field, 78
Spirit of St. Louis, 44, 78, 90, 92
Sports and Recreation, 4-6, 63, 103
Spreckels, Adolph, 86
Spreckels, John D., 42, 49, 69, 86
Spreckels Organ, 86
Spreckels Organ Pavilion, 86
Spring Valley, 123

"Squibob, John Q.", pseudonym of G. H. Derby, 40
Squibob Papers, by G. H. Derby, 40
Stadii: city stadium, 67, 90; Aztec Bowl, 112
Star of India (ship museum), 95
Star, San Diego, 120
State Building, 86
State College, San Diego, 61, 112
State Normal School, 67
State Societies, 58
Stearns, Abel, 31
Steel boat, 93
Stephens Collection of Birds and Mammals, 89
Stephenson's Regiment, 36
Stewart, John C., 78
Stewart, Casa de, 78
Stockton, Robert F., Comdr., 34, 72, 75
Stonewall Jackson (mine), 116
Stonington (ship), 34
Streetcar and bus service, 1-2
Street order and numbering, 7
Sud-California Deutsche Zeitung, 60
Sun, The San Diego, 42, 60
Sunset Cliffs, 80, 95
Sutherland Dam fiasco, 69
Sweetwater Lake and Dam, 42, 48, 124
Sweetwater River, 124

Table Mountain, 101
Tamia, K., 88
Tasta, Fausto, 62
Taxis, 1
Tecate, 125
Telegraph Canyon, 124
Temecula Valley, 122
Temperature, 18
Tent City, 101-102
Texas and Pacific Railroad, 42
Theosophical Society, 62
Thum Park, 117
Tijuana, 100
Tijuana River, 100
Tingley, Mme. Katherine, 80
Todos Santos Bay, 101
Topography, 17, 18, 19
Torrey Pines Mesa, 98
Torrey Pines Park, 103
Town Council, first, 64
Traders and settlers, American, 30-31
Traffic regulations, 3
Transportation, 40, 42, 48-50, 53
Traveler (ship), 64
Tres Reyes (ship), 25
Tribune, Evening, 42, 60, 67
Truman, Ben, Major, 40
Tuna clippers, 57
Turkey Day Festival, 116
Two Years Before the Mast, by R. H. Dana, Jr., 30, 107

Ubach, Fr. Antonio, 76, 77

Union, The San Diego, 41, 42, 60, 66, 76
Union - Tribune Southern Electrical Broadcasting Co., 68
United Air Lines Depot, 90
United States Government establishments, see under definitive names
Upper Otay Lake and Dam, 48, 125
U. S. Grant Hotel, 41

Valentin, 125
Valle de San Jose, 121
Vallecito Stage Station, 120-121
Vallecito Valley, 114, 120
Valley Center, 112
Vancouver, George, Capt., 82
Vargas, Manuel de, 64
Victoria (ship), 24
Victoria, Manuel, Gov., 31-32
Viejas Indian Reservation, 113
Vista, 105
Vizcaino, Sebastian, 14, 25, 82
Vizcaino Marker, 82
Volcan Mountain, 122, 123

Wade, Leigh, 69
Warner, J. J., 121
Warner Ranch, 121-122
Warner Springs, 39, 122
Warner Stage Station, 120, 121
Warner Valley, 121
Water development, 38, 42, 45, 46-48, 53, 67, 69
Waterfront: points of interest, 90-95
Weather Bureau, U. S., 90
Whaley, Thomas, 76
Whaley House, 76
Whaling industry, 46
Whaling station, 82
White, Stanford, 102
White Star, 126
White, Stewart E., 80
Wilbur, Curtis, 69
Wild Flower Protection, 3
Willows, the, 113
Winslow, Carlton, 96
Wishing Well, 86
Wister, Owen, 60
Witch Creek, 116
Wolfskill Ranch, 106
Works Progress Administration, 50, 77
World, The, 46
Wright, Harold Bell, 60, 106
Wynola, 116

Yachting, 63
Yankee traders, 31
Yankee visitors, first, 28
Y. M. C. A., 66

Zamorano, Agustin V., 32
Zoo, San Diego (Zoological Garden), 88-89
Zoonooz, 61